SINGLES
Ministry Resources

Discovering
God's Design
ON YOUR LIFE

Lana Wilkinson

David C. Cook

Dedicated to...
The singles at Casas Adobes Baptist Church—they are so excited about this book. I asked the small group leaders to recruit folks to hang around and brainstorm interactive options ideas with me one Sunday afternoon. I was blown away when 20 faces appeared! It is to those young men and women, and the work God is doing through them, that I lovingly dedicate these pages:

Jack and Lee Delyria (and their boys, Kyle and Tyler), Gerald Barrett, Jr., Caron Browder, Marta Burgess, Jennifer Calkins, Sonia Carranza, Steve Davies, Laura Davis, John McGehee, Rich Ormand, Carlina Persons, Bill Potts, Emily Potts, Amy Price, Sara Ridenour, Paul Short, Lois Simpson, Keith Skogen, Phil Stairs.

Discovering God's Design on Your Life
© 1998 David C. Cook Church Ministries, a division of Cook Communications Ministries

Cable address: DCCOOK
Series creator: Jerry Jones
Series editor: Gary Wilde
Designer: Joanna Shafer
Cover illustrator: Don Pierce

Unless otherwise noted, Scripture quotations are from the Holy Bible, New International Version (NIV), ©1973, 1978, 1984 by International Bible Society. Used by permission of Zondervan Bible Publishers.

Published by Cook Communications Ministries
4050 Lee Vance View
Colorado Springs, CO 80918

Printed in U.S.A.

ISBN: 0-7814-5464-6

CONTENTS

About Me—the Author

Lana Wilkinson—I began working in single adult ministry as a single parent in 1976. The only "gifts" I knew I had were the "gift of mouth" and the "gift of instigation." Both had gotten me in trouble on more than one occasion. I also knew that the Lord had chosen me to inform my church's pastors about the unmet needs of single parents such as myself. With their blessing, I initiated and organized a ministry to single parents. It quickly grew to exceed 100 in attendance.

There were no books to read about how to minister with single parents. My pastors didn't have a clue. I had no training. But God had work that He wanted done and the Holy Spirit revealed the "what" and the "how" to me.

Since then, my passion has been to know how God calls and equips His children—and to communicate those principles to others who get involved in His work and, in turn, mentor others. God has opened many doors for building ministries, writing, and speaking over these 20 years.

Today, my husband Jerry and I both serve on staff with Casas Adobes Baptist Church in Tucson, Arizona. Jerry is Minister with Single Adults; I am Coordinator of Volunteer Involvement. God has even arranged for me to draw a salary from teaching folks how God calls and equips them. Isn't He good?

WELCOME TO...
An exciting study experience with your singles!

We think you've made an excellent choice with Single Adult Ministry Studies leader's guides. In this series, you have a *single focus* with *multiple options* format, designed to build healthy relationships and deal with relevant topics for today's single adults—all from a biblical perspective.

The concept for this series is the result of in-depth explorations with singles ministry leaders from across the country. In focus groups and one-on-one interviews, these experts "on the front lines" of single adult Christian education told us what they need and want for their groups. As a result, you get the most practical activities and the most relevant, up-to-date discussions of constantly requested topics.

The volumes in this series are for singles groups from every age group, background, denomination, and life situation. We've targeted, in particular, single adults ages 25-32 (although we fully expect that this series will be enjoyed by older singles, as well). No matter who is in your group, make everyone feel welcomed and appreciated. And use your session plans as the springboard for genuine, open communication and discussion.

Using This Guide

You'll soon realize that SAM Studies are extremely flexible and adaptable to your particular needs. That's because the three Instruction Pages in each session let you plan for a variety of time frames and settings:

- A "Short Course—as in a Sunday school Bible study (35-45 minutes); or
- A Small Group Setting—either in a home or as a "break out" from a larger group (60-90 minutes); or
- A Large Group Setting—for an Extended Weeknight Program or Retreat Setting (two hours or more).

Singles ministry leaders have indicated again and again that they want the material to be easy to use in any one of these three settings. After all, volunteers are often leading the group—people who may not take the time to read the entire course. These leaders often just want the material for the meeting they are responsible for. As a result, this series is designed to make preparation as complete and organized as possible. It all begins with becoming familiar with how each session is put together...

Session Intro / Overview Page. This is your introduction to the study topic, giving you an interest-grabbing overview, Session Aim, Key Concepts, and Bible References.

Instruction Pages. Here you'll find three different sets of instructions, depending on the size, setting, and time requirements of your particular group. Choose the session that's best for you!

My Personal Game Plan. This is your personal session-planning page. It helps you organize the activities and options you've chosen, step by step. It also includes "Just for You"—a short devotional exercise to prepare your own heart for leading the session.

Looking to the Word. This step lays out the key themes that should flow from your time together. It's actually a mini-lecture that is "presentation based"—given to you exactly as you might present it to your group. Of course, you'll want to make it your own by studying it thoroughly and adding personal anecdotes and illustrations to make it sing!

This section includes Going Deeper. It provides informative "nuggets" related to the textual, cultural, or historical background of the Bible passages. The singles ministry leaders we interviewed said: "Give me information that helps me look like an expert."

"Extra Options" Pages or **"Extra Info" Pages.** In sessions 1, 4, and 6, these two pages list several **acvitivy options** to use in your teaching plan. Go here when you're looking for a broader range of active alternatives for group participation. In sessions 2, 3, and 5, these pages give you **extra information** to deliver in the form of an additional handout, front and back. Photocopy these pages and use them with students as important assessment tools.

(IMPORTANT NOTE: The inventories and assessment sheets in each session all lead up to the final handout in Session 6, titled: "My SHAPE for Service," on page 91. Review that handout before you begin this course, and take note of the various handouts in each session that students will need to complete in order to fill in this last one for themselves.)

Reproducible Interactive Pages. These are your reproducible handouts, to be used by group members during the session. Interactive Page #1 goes with the short meeting time setting. Interactive Page #2 goes with the small group setting. You'll find group activities, individual exercises, and discussion questions here.

Take Home Page (front and back). Use this page as a kind of bulletin insert that group members can take home with them. It will help "set the hook" on the Key Concepts you've conveyed during your session. Occasionally, it will also offer activities to be used in the session itself.

So...once you know how everything's organized, you'll lead your group through five steps in each session. These steps are clearly laid out on the Instruction Page you choose for your group and setting.

Take Note!

Pay special attention to these items in your SAM leader's guide, and become familiar with how to use them in the most effective ways.

- **About the Options.** Feel free to insert them wherever you think they'd work the best for you. The idea is for you to build a lesson plan from the "menu of methods" we've provided. Go for it!

- **About the Icons.** Notice that the icons on the Instruction Pages visually coordinate with the Interactive Pages you'll use them with. Just another way to help you stay organized.

• **About the "Extra Info" Pages.** Use these as additional handouts. Note that the inventories and assessment sheets in each session *all lead up to the final handout in Session 6, titled: "My SHAPE for Service,"* on page 91. **It's important that you review that handout before you begin this course,** and take note of the various handouts in each session that students will need to complete in order to fill in this last one for themselves.

• **About the Take Home Pages.** You'll photocopy these pages for everyone—back-to-back, if possible, to make a single handout sheet. That way, group members can fold them and use them as an insert in their Bibles during the week ahead.

• **About "Presenting What the Bible Has to Say."** We want you to be an expert presenter during the Bible content portion of your session. That's why we give you the outlines and illustrations you can use to make everything flow in a smooth and interesting mini-talk. Just go over the material thoroughly and adjust it here and there to truly make it your own.

Not Just Theory

*D*iscovering God's Design on Your Life is no ivory tower theory. It really can transform lives and ministries. Let me share an example. Primetime, our 20-something singles' ministry, was struggling. They averaged barely over a dozen in Sunday morning Bible study. Their teacher, Jack Delyria, and his wife, Lee, were awesome. The singles were sharp young men and women—but they avoided involvement. They arrived in groups of two or three, sat five chairs away from the next two or three, and few even knew each others' names. It just wasn't happening.

Jack and Lee invited me to conduct the six-week workshop on Spiritual gifts, Heart, Abilities, Personal style and Experiences that Jerry and I wrote for Casas. We call it "S.H.A.P.E."; you're about to study its principles. I taught the class for six weeks. We identified gifts and personal styles and plugged people in where the Lord had designed them to serve. We prayed for an administrator; the Lord brought one.

A year has passed. Primetime now runs 40 or so young single adults (and growing!) on Sundays. The atmosphere is electric. Folks greet each other; some lead music; others bring refreshments, make announcements, and keep records. They have a full calendar of activities and lead three dynamic midweek small groups. They do community service. They have planned a retreat; both the college and the 30-something singles' classes are invited. They're doing it all themselves. I just stop by now and then to answer questions, collect hugs, and cheer!

Other Books in the SAM Studies series—

Living in an Uncertain World (Studies in the Book of Ruth)
Building Community
Living Your Faith Inside and Out

To Order, call: 1-888-888-4SAM.

Session 1

Invest Here!
(AWESOME RETURNS)

Our world tells us that we work to make money ... to buy things ... that will make us happy. Our senses are assaulted—and our intelligence insulted—by incredible promises: "Buy *this*, and all will be wonderful!"

But all is not wonderful. Smiling faces mask shattered lives all around us. Purchased pleasures often addict and destroy. "Maybe work is the problem," some reason, and drop out of the "system." Others live like hamsters on a treadmill— running full speed and getting nowhere.

"Will I ever find real worth and happiness?" we wonder. "Or is life just a series of infomercials that never perform as advertised?" We all seek direction for our lives. Searching for happiness and fulfillment, we often accept temporary gratification and enduring emptiness.

But here's the good news: God places direction *within us!* He designs us with purpose. As we discover who He has designed us to be, we understand what we can do to find true happiness and fulfillment.

Single adults today need to know that worth and happiness are not found in the acquisition of the next gadget— or the next relationship. True worth and happiness flow from investing the resources God has placed in us, in order to do the work He has uniquely designed us to do.

SESSION AIM

To help single adults recognize that they are created for service and that fulfillment flows from serving according to God's design.

WHAT'S IT ALL ABOUT?

As you move through your session, keep in mind these Key Concepts you'll be conveying to your group members:

• Knowing Jesus means a call to service.
• God prepares our work according to our abilities.
• We need to invest what He gives us.
• As we faithfully invest, God gives us more to manage.
• Happiness is a byproduct of investing ourselves in service.

BIBLE REFERENCES:

Matthew 20:20-21, 24-28.
Matthew 25:14-15, 19-28, 30
Ephesians 2:10
James 2:14-26

9

Your 'Short Course' Set-Up...
(How to Use This Material in 35-45 Minutes)
Example: Sunday Morning Bible Study

1—Let's Get Started
(5-10 minutes)

Option 1: Different Designs, Different Functions
Needed: Interactive Page #1, pencils.

Distribute Interactive Page #1 and form small groups. Direct attention to the exercise titled "Different Designs, Different Functions," and have the group members read the instructions and get started filling in blanks and then discussing the questions. Encourage creativity! (Vehicles could range from a child's toy to a space ship; famous people, from biblical characters to professional wrestlers.) Time permitting, ask the groups to share their funniest or most disastrous switched-function results with the balance of the class.

Option 2: Thought-Starter Questions

Launch your session by having partners or small groups answer the questions below. You may wish to write them on chalkboard or newsprint.

- *Describe two things you enjoy doing and do reasonably well. Tell why you enjoy them.*
- *What skills or interests make this activity fun for you?*
- *To what extent do you see your particular skills as "gifts" from God? Explain.*

Note: If time or interest allows, use additional options found on pages 17-18.

2—Looking to the Word
(15 minutes)

1. Explain that this study examines how God purposefully designs us and then provides happiness and fulfillment as we serve according to His design.
2. Gather everyone for "Presenting What the Bible Has to Say," found on pages 14-16. Prepare this mini-talk ahead of time, blending in your own life experiences and personal illustrations. Make this presentation your own!

3—Applying It to My Life
(5-10 minutes)

Needed: Interactive Page #1, pencils.

As soon as you complete your presentation, get individuals started working on the exercise titled "Evaluate Your SQ" on Interactive Page #1. After several minutes, ask volunteers to talk about:

- *What is the most difficult thing about applying the Key Concepts—in practical ways— to our lives today?*

4—Taking the Next Step
(5 minutes)

Needed: Take Home Page, pencils.

1. Distribute the Take Home Page. Then ask: "Do you recall why the one servant buried his talent?" (The obvious answer is: "He was afraid.") Remind your group members that the master expected this servant to make at least a safe, low-interest investment. Then ask:

- *Why do we sometimes hesitate to invest the resources we have been given? What are our own fears today?*

2. Now have everyone read and privately respond to "Bringing the Lesson Home" on the Take Home Page.

5—Let's Wrap It Up
(5 minutes)

1. Make your group's announcements at this time.
2. Use the Extra Option titled "Looking Ahead," completing the acronym with your students: Spiritual gifts, Heart's desires, Abilities, Personal style, and Experiences.
3. Close by seeking God's blessing and revelation for each person in the group, as you seek to better understand His plan for your lives.

When You Have More Time...
(How to Use This Material in 60-90 Minutes)
Example: Small Groups at Home

1—Let's Get Started
(5-10 minutes)

Option 1: The Business Plan
Needed: Interactive Page #2, pencils.

Form groups of three to four people and distribute Interactive Page #2. Have groups read the scenario under "The Business Plan" and then brainstorm to complete Part 1, then discuss Part 2. Call for a sharing of insights before you move into your mini-lecture.

Option 2: Describe a Servant
In small groups of three or four, have group members describe a Christian they know who exhibits joy in serving. Ask:

•*What does the person do? What abilities does he or she use to do the job well?*
•*What would it take for you, personally, to have more joy in your daily work? in your ability to serve others?*

2—Looking to the Word
(10-15 minutes)

1. Explain that today's study examines how God purposefully designs us and then provides happiness and fulfillment as we serve according to His design.
2. Present the material found in "Presenting What the Bible Has to Say," on pages 14-16. Divide your allotted time into three segments: (1) Introduction, (2) Key Concepts, and (3) Conclusion. Keep your presentation short and simple. Hit the highlights, drawing upon the "Going Deeper" information as appropriate.

3—Applying It to My Life
(20-25 minutes)

Once you complete your presentation, use either Option 1 or or Option 2 below, depending on how you launched your session:

Option 1: Business Plan Redux
Follow the instructions for this activity, as found in the Extra Options section, page 17.

Option 2: Quote Reactions
Needed: Take Home Page.

If you started with the second opener, do a quote-reaction exercise related to the statement by Frederick Buechner in "In Other Words" on the Take Home Page. Have partners or small groups read the quote and then develop responses to:

•*Do you agree or disagree with this statement? Why?*
•*What personal illustration from your life seems to affirm or deny this quote?*
•*How would you rewrite this quotation to make it more relevant to your unique experience?*

4—Taking the Next Step
(15-20 minutes)

Needed: Interactive Page #2, pencils.

Have small groups work on the activity titled "Fighting Over the Presents?" Stress that you are looking for true-to-life examples of how "gift jealousy" can hinder effective ministry. Ask everyone to be very practical and specific about how this problem can be solved. Call for a sharing of insights with the whole group (from designated small-group "reporters").

5—Let's Wrap It Up
(10-20 minutes)

1. Make your group's announcements and encourage everyone to read through the Take Home Page during the coming week.
2. Spend some moments in silence, asking everyone to reflect on their personal response to the session's theme. Then ask the Lord to pour out His insights upon the individuals in your group during the coming weeks. Ask also for His blessings on the friendships that will be growing as you study and seek understanding together.

HINT:

Leader Preparation.
Plan the timing of each step on your "Game Plan" worksheet. Allow 2-3 minutes per response for discussion and interaction. Expect everything to take more time than planned; don't plan too much. Have a back-up option or two ready in the rare event that discussions move more quickly than anticipated.

11

1 — Let's Get Started
(20-30 minutes)

Option 1: Which Part Am I?
Needed: Paper, markers or crayons.

Form small groups and remind everyone that the Bible describes Christians as the Body of Christ. Some church members are the hands, others feet, eyes, ears, etc. Give each group member a blank sheet of paper and a marker. Ask them to (1) draw the parts of Christ's body they might represent, and (2) explain to the group *why* they have chosen those parts.

Option 2: Agree or Disagree?
Tell your singles that you are going to read a series of "controversial" statements. After reading each one, ask for a show of hands indicating whether people agree or disagree with the statement. Use the statements as the basis for a discussion on the nature of discerning our God-given abilities. The statements are:

- God never asks us to do something without equipping us first.
- We shouldn't attempt to do a ministry unless we're certain we have the gifts for it.
- If we have a certain gift for service, we will always be aware of it.
- Knowing our purpose in life is always a life-long process of discernment.
- We can never be absolutely certain we are doing God's will.
- Sometimes, we need to invest in ourselves instead of others.

Tell students that you expect to grapple with these kinds of issues now, and in future sessions. Then move to your mini-lecture.

2 — Looking to the Word
(35 minutes)

1. Explain that today's study examines how God purposefully designs us and then provides happiness and fulfillment as we serve according to His design.
2. Offer a brief mini-lecture using the material found in "Presenting What the Bible Has to Say," on pages 14-16.

3 — Applying It to My Life
(30 minutes)

1. When you're through presenting "Looking to the Word," use the exercise titled "Evaluate Your SQ" on Interactive Page #1 and ask volunteers to talk about:

- *What is the most difficult thing about applying the Key Concepts—in practical ways— to our lives today?*

2. If you will have time, follow up with small groups working on the activity titled "Fighting Over the Presents?"

4 — Taking the Next Step
(40 minutes)
Needed: Take Home Page.

1. For groups who know each other well. Form small groups of three or four people. Have participants take turns affirming for each group member: (1) what tasks he or she does well that are appreciated by the others, and (2) what personal traits make each person special to the others.
2. For newer groups, use the activity on the Take Home Page titled: "Bring the Lesson Home." Let each person work in silence, and suggest silent prayer until all are finished responding.

5 — Let's Wrap It Up
(5 minutes)

Close in prayer by using one of these methods (your choice!):

___ Focus on one key concern of the group or a group member, and all pray about that concern, as led.
___ Spend moments in silent prayer.
___ Assign specific requests to people before bowing for prayer.
___ One volunteer prays, covering issues and concerns raised.
___ Everyone prays for the person on his or her right.
___ Lay hands on a person who expresses need, and focus on that situation.
___ Sing the doxology, or a praise chorus.
___ Pray sentence prayers, with a designated closer.

HINT:

Think "relationship." Jesus invested a large part of his ministry energy in twelve persons. Optimal spiritual growth occurs among Christians who know each other well and who invest energy in each other's lives. As you plan for this and the next five two-hour sessions, remember: RELATIONSHIP! RELATIONSHIP! RELATIONSHIP!

My Personal Game Plan

STEP 1 Time: _____ minutes.

Materials Needed:

Activities Summary:

STEP 2 Time: _____ minutes.

Materials Needed:

Activities Summary:

STEP 3 Time: _____ minutes.

Materials Needed:

Activities Summary:

STEP 4 Time: _____ minutes.

Materials Needed:

Activities Summary:

STEP 5 Time: _____ minutes.

Materials Needed:

Activities Summary:

Just for You
Teacher's Devotional

The apostle Peter encouraged elders, "Be shepherds of God's flock that is under your care, serving as overseers—not because you must, but because you are willing, as God wants you to be; ... eager to serve;...being examples to the flock. And when the Chief Shepherd appears, you will receive the crown of glory that will never fade away" (from 1 Pet. 5:2-4).

Shepherd God's flock of single adults He has entrusted to you! Help them to better understand His design on their lives. And celebrate His calling on your life. What a privilege it is to be a servant-leader!

Leadership development expert John Maxwell writes, "God's gift to me is my potential. My gift back to God is what I do with that potential. I believe great leaders sense a 'higher calling'—one that lifts them above themselves."*

What would it take for you to receive with open arms the "higher calling" of motivating the men and women God has entrusted to you? What would it take to be a "great leader" of your flock? For starters, why not begin to ...

• Smile as they start understanding who God created them to be.
• Cheer as they apply their "being" to their "doing."
• Celebrate as they experience God's power surging through their lives.

Be assured that God will reward you for your faithfulness. You have His Word on it!

—Lana Wilkinson

* John C. Maxwell, *Developing the Leader Within You* (Nashville: Thomas Nelson Publishers, 1993).

MY GOALS FOR THIS SESSION:

- TO HELP SINGLE ADULTS
  _____
  _____
  _____
- TO HELP SINGLE ADULTS
  _____
  _____
  _____
- TO HELP SINGLE ADULTS
  _____
  _____
  _____
- TO HELP SINGLE ADULTS
  _____
  _____
  _____

WHAT I LEARNED FROM READING 'LOOKING TO THE WORD'...

Notes and Insights—

13

Presenting
What the Bible Has to Say...

Here's your mini-lecture covering the biblical Key Concepts. Try to become familiar with the flow of thoughts, and the outline, in order to present this material with maximum eye contact. Special instructions to you are in bold type.

Introduction

Someone has said: "The moment you stop living on purpose you start dying by accident." Do you agree? I believe that single adults today need to know that their purpose—their worth and happiness—are not found in the world's system of accumulation and self-gratification. True worth and happiness flow from investing the resources God has placed in us to do the work He has uniquely designed us to do.

Transition Statement: How do we do it? Let's look at some of the "Key Principles of Heavenly Investing"...

• Knowing Jesus means a call to service.
• God prepares our work according to our abilities.
• We need to invest what He gives us.
• As we faithfully invest, God gives us more to manage.
• Happiness is a byproduct of investing ourselves in service.

KEY CONCEPT #1:
Knowing Jesus means a call to service.

Have someone read aloud Ephesians 2:10. Ask:

• *What do you think Paul means when he says, "Created in Christ Jesus to do good works"?*

We are unique creatures, created to do good works, which God prepared for us to do. Neither our abilities, nor the works we are to do, are without purpose. The point is: Our relationship with Jesus *automatically* includes a call to service.

Most of us are aware of this call in our lives. What is it for you? The tough part is that we all "Know" more than we "Do."

Illustration. The young preacher thrilled his congregation with his first sermon—a challenge to "gird their loins" for Christian service and living. Then, to their dismay, he preached the same sermon the following Sunday. When he confronted them with the same ringing message on the third Sunday, the people felt something must be done.

"Don't you have more than just one sermon?" blurted a spokesman to the pastor.

"Oh, yes," he said quietly. "I have quite a number. But you haven't done anything about the first one yet!"

KEY CONCEPT #2:
God prepares our work according to our abilities.

Have someone read aloud The Parable of the Talents in Matthew 25:14-30. Then ask:

• *How did the master decide which servant would be trusted with one, two, or five talents?*

We Christians are to be good managers of much more than our finances. We are to be stewards of everything we possess: our time, talents, gifts, relationships, bodies, minds, hearts, actions, thoughts, and material resources. The master gave responsibility to each servant "according to his ability." The master knew his servants. He knew who was capable of a greater or lesser level of responsibility.

Yes, God prepares work for us to do according to the abilities He has given us.

• *Have you ever "gotten in over your head" by consenting to do something—then finding your abilities falling short? How did you handle that situation?*

Illustration. The apostle Paul said, in Ephesians 1:7: "In him we have redemption through his blood, the forgiveness of sins, in accordance with the riches of God's grace." *According to* His riches. Thank God, he did not say *out of* His riches," which would be like a millionaire giving $1.00 in the offering plate, as it would be "out of" his riches. "According to" means "in proportion to"—and God's proportionate provisions come without measure.

KEY CONCEPT #3:
We need to invest what He gives us.

God expects us to invest what He gives us. The master gave an identical commendation to both the five-talent man and the two-talent man. In contrast, he was angry with the one-talent man because he didn't even attempt to invest what had been entrusted to him. All the master expected any of them to do was to risk investing what they had been given—even if the rate of return was minimal.

•*Why was the master pleased with the 5-talent and 10-talent servants and angry with the one-talent servant?*

Two truths often are missed in the study of this passage: (1) part of the reward was sharing the master's happiness, and (2) part of the punishment was emotional anguish. The master said to the two investors, "Come and share your master's happiness." The one who did not invest was thrown out where there would be "weeping and gnashing of teeth."

Don't miss this. Some of the unhappiest, most negative individuals in the world are Christians who refuse to invest the resources God has entrusted to them. The Holy Spirit within them reveals work that needs to be done. He urges them to use what they have been given and do that work. But instead of rolling up their sleeves and getting busy, they whine, complain, and criticize because somebody else is not doing what they know needs to be done. Misunderstanding the nature of God, they fear loss if they invest their resources. They fail to realize that He will give them everything they need to do the job. Sadly, they do not understand the principle that we give up trinkets and receive treasure in return!

KEY CONCEPT #4:
As we faithfully invest, God gives us more to manage.

What the two servants did resulted in increased authority. When we faithfully invest what we are given, God gives us more to manage. Notice that the master didn't just praise the work of the two investors. Because they were faithful with what he had entrusted to them, he gave them more authority to act on his behalf.

Illustration. The great violinist Nicolo Paganini willed his marvelous violin to the city of Genoa, on condition that it must never again be played upon. Wood, while used and handled, wears but slightly. Discarded it begins to decay. The lovely toned violin has become wormeaten and useless. It is only a reminder that a life withdrawn from service to others becomes quite useless.

Have someone read aloud James 2:14-26.

The point is: faith must issue in work!
The writer of James was not the disciple James, but the younger half-brother of Jesus. James emphasizes not just believing the right things, but following through with right behavior.
During Jesus' lifetime, James resisted putting his faith in his older brother (see John 7:5). After His resurrection, Jesus personally appeared to James (1 Cor. 15:7). James joined the believers who awaited the outpouring of the Holy Spirit (Acts 1:14) and became a leader in the Jerusalem church (Acts 15:13). What better qualified witness than the brother of Jesus to assert, "Walk your talk. If you don't act like who you say you are, then something is wrong with what you say you believe!"

HINT:

When planning your lesson for any time frame, build your foundation from the Five Key Concepts. Teach one principle at a time, using a back and forth style by asking an occasional question. Add building blocks to the foundation according to the time frame and the needs and preferences of your group.

The encouraging thing is that Jesus told the disciples *how* to be great, rather than condemning their desire to achieve greatness. We can have legitimate aspirations, dreams, and goals in our lives. Jesus is there to affirm and strengthen us as we work toward worthy accomplishments in our lives.

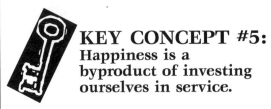

KEY CONCEPT #5: Happiness is a byproduct of investing ourselves in service.

Read aloud Matthew 20:20-21, 24-28.

In countless ways, Jesus demonstrated and explained a lifestyle of serving—but the disciples often simply do not understand. They still ask, "What's in this for me? How will I be given recognition?"

Jesus does not condemn James and John's desire to be recognized, nor the others for being indignant. Instead, He gathers these men together and explains that true greatness can be achieved—but only through being a servant. Whoever desires to be first, Jesus says, must be a slave of all.

Conclusion

Slightly more than a week later, these men fled in terror as Jesus was crucified. Yet after His resurrection, Jesus charged them with taking His message to the world. Previously confused, quarreling and afraid, they set aside their differences and boldly began serving and demonstrating their faith. What transformed them from fearful followers to fearless servant-leaders? What will transform *you* in the same way?

GOING DEEPER

Notes on Ephesians 2:10. Paul is writing from Rome, where he has been under house arrest for about a year. Five years earlier, in a letter to the church at Corinth, Paul had described the hardships he had endured for the Gospel (2 Cor. 11:11). He had been whipped, beaten, stoned and shipwrecked; in danger from rivers, bandits, Jews, Gentiles, and false Christians in the city, in the country and at sea. He had been sleepless, hungry, thirsty, cold and naked. So how could he rejoice in these "good works, which God prepared in advance for [him] to do"? (see Phil. 4:4, 6-7).

No doubt it was because he knew that he was doing what God had called him to do. He was certain of his calling. He knew the abilities God had given him. He understood God's workmanship.

As God's workmanship, we have been given all the raw materials required to do everything He has designed us to do. As we use what we have been given, He continues to mold us—strengthening our skills, polishing our perceptions, revealing our purposes one step at a time.

As we are faithful in serving according to His design, we, like Paul, are able to rejoice even in the middle of life's hardships. We develop an awesome understanding that we are purposefully created by God Almighty.

Our relationships with others in the body of Christ are improved as we understand that they, too, are purposefully designed. We can give each other room to grow as we recall the adage, "Please be patient. God isn't finished with me, yet."

Notes on Matthew 25:14-15, 19-28, 30. Matthew wrote an eyewitness account of Jesus' life. He had been a tax collector when Jesus walked up to his booth one day and said, "Follow me" (Matt. 9:9). Matthew closed his business and followed.

The Gospel of Matthew gives in-depth counsel on the wise use of money, including giving secretly, supporting aged parents, and paying laborers. As one whose previous vocation had focused on finances, Matthew was well aware of the link between our hearts and our pocketbooks.

The Parable of the Talents was part of a series of parables Jesus taught to His disciples on the Mount of Olives, two days before his arrest and trial. Perhaps this parable made a strong impression on Matthew as he realized the value of the trust placed in these servants by the master. One drachma was about a day's wages; one mina equaled 100 drachmas; one talent equaled 60 minas. If we do our calculations counting a six-day work week and two weeks of vacation, that one buried talent was worth 20 years' wages!

No doubt this ex-tax collector's mental calculator was working overtime, as Jesus described the master's entrusting 200 years' worth of wages to one servant, 100 to a second, and 20 to a third! "What an astronomical sum," he must have reckoned.

EXTRA OPTIONS

Pick and Choose any of the following to fit the needs of your group...

You are here

Options to Consider...for Step 1

Missing Pieces—In advance, prepare one five-minute-solution children's jigsaw puzzle for every five participants. Remove a few key pieces from each puzzle, then place the puzzles in separate plastic bags without a picture of the completed scene.

Form small groups of five or six people. Give a bag to each group. Instruct them to work the puzzle and then wait for further instructions. When they discover that pieces are missing, act surprised. They must be kidding! Then become indignant. Blame the manufacturer? When sufficient turmoil ensues, confess that you removed the pieces.

Relate the puzzle's picture to the work of the church, and its pieces to God's people. Ask groups to discuss:

•What happens to the work of the church when "pieces" are missing?

•Why do we often find that "pieces" are missing in the ministry of the church? What can be done about it?

Options to Consider...for Step 3

Business Plan Redux—This option ties back into "The Business Plan" opener.
Needed: In advance, prepare a large poster with wording described below.

Ask participants to regroup with their "Business Plan" group from Step 1. Then display a poster with the following:

•Business Partners=God
  (Father, Son and Holy Spirit)
•Restaurant=The Church
•Investment=Jesus' life
•Product=Meeting needs by
  serving with love
•Profit=Changed lives (those
  serving/being served)
•Job descriptions=The works
  Christians are to do
•Employees=You and your group
•Abilities=Resources God has
  given you
•Bonuses=_____

Say: "We have been studying how God equips us to do what He calls us to do. Let's apply that to ourselves, personally. Look back at the opening exercise, 'The Business Plan,' Interactive Page #2."

Give instructions 1 and 2 below; allow time to complete individually. Then, state instructions 3 through 5 and allow discussion. Close with instruction 6.

Instructions:
1. Substitute the poster's words for those underlined on your sheet.
2. What bonuses do we receive for faithfully doing our jobs? (Clue: Key Concepts 4 and 5.)
3. Substitute group members' names for the employee names.
4. Discuss work each person might do to serve others.
5. What abilities/resources would each use?
6. Discuss Part two in light of this new scenario.

Topical Brainstorm
Needed: Colored poster boards or butcher papers; felt markers.

Write one of these titles on each poster:

17

HINT:

To minimize time requirements in "Talk-It-Over" settings, ask for feedback from the whole class; allow three minutes per question in your planning time. To maximize interaction among classmates, break up into small groups and allow three minutes per person per question.

RESOURCES TO INVEST
SERVICE OPPORTUNITIES
FEARS THAT INHIBIT
ATTITUDES FOR SUCCESS

Form the class into four groups, each with a poster and marker. Have them brainstorm and list words or phrases relating each of their topics to Christian service. After a few minutes, have the groups read aloud their posters in the order listed above.

Options to Consider…for Step 4

The Gift of Affirmation—For groups who know each other well. Form small groups. Have participants take turns affirming for each group member (1) what tasks he or she does well that are appreciated by the others, and (2) what personal traits make each person special to the others.

A Note of Thanx—In advance, bring scratch paper, blank note cards and envelopes for each person in class. Ask participants to think of some person whose service they appreciate—a parent, family member, friend, church leader, coworker, etc. Have them write a note of thanks to the individual, expressing appreciation both for the task *and the traits* of the person they are writing.

Options to Consider…for Step 5

Sing a Fun Song—Check with a children's music leader in your church, browse your local Christian book store, or watch children's television programs for simple songs that affirm individual uniqueness. Learn a fun song and teach it to your group. Involve your primary "instigators," who will easily get into the fun and help others to relax and enjoy the freedom of "being a kid."

Looking Ahead—Use this as a way to spark interest in the next week's session.

Say: Over the course of this study, we will look at how God forms each of us with unique combinations of attributes, which form our "SHAPE" for service. Then fill in the acrostic together:

S_____ Gifts—The "what" we do in ministry.

H_____'s Desires—The "where" we do our ministry.

A_____- Our physical, mental, and emotional resources.

P_____ Style—Our unique way of relating to ourselves and to others.

E_____—How God instructs, matures and fine-tunes all of the above!

(Responses: Spiritual gifts, Heart's desires, Abilities, Personal style, and Experiences)

Closing Prayer—For groups who know each other well. Have each group member offer a short prayer, thanking God for one specific thing about the person to his or her right and requesting a blessing for them during the coming week.

DIFFERENT DESIGNS, DIFFERENT FUNCTIONS

Take turns going around your circle, naming and filling in one blank at a time. Maximize the fun! Think of out-of-the-ordinary vehicles and strikingly different people—and don't duplicate anybody else's selections. When everyone's blanks are filled, talk through the two discussion questions that follow.

• Name three very different kinds of transportation vehicles:

_____   _____   _____

• Name three people who are famous in very different arenas:

_____   _____   _____

•*Think about the function each vehicle or person performs. What special qualities fit their tasks?*
•*What funny or disastrous results could occur if they switched functions? How would their job be missed if it were not done?*

FOOD FOR THOUGHT: Replace one of the famous people you named above with your name. Answer the discussion questions about yourself.

KEY CONCEPTS
on Investing Your Life

#1 Knowing Jesus means a _____ to _____.
#2 God _____ our work according to our _____.
#3 We need to _____ what He _____ us.
#4 As we faithfully invest, God _____ us more to _____.
#5 _____ is a _____ of investing ourselves in service.

EVALUATE YOUR SQ*

1. Which of the servants in the Parable am I most like?_____

2. How would I rank my awareness of the spiritual gifts, abilities, and personal style God has given me for ministry?
   0_____1_____2_____3_____4_____5
   Clueless   **Got it Wired**

3. How would I rank the opportunities for service in my world?
   0_____1_____2_____3_____4_____5
   Nothing to Do   **Overwhelming Need**

4. To what degree am I responding to the needs around me?
   0_____1_____2_____3_____4_____5
   Standing Still   **Burned Out**

5. The one thing God seems to be calling me to do these days is...

*Service Quotient

Then the mother of Zebedee's sons came to Jesus with her sons and, kneeling down, asked a favor of him. 21 "What is it you want?" he asked. She said, "Grant that one of these two sons of mine may sit at your right and the other at your left in your kingdom."… 24 When the ten heard about this, they were indignant with the two brothers. 25 Jesus called them together and said, "You know that the rulers of the Gentiles lord it over them, and their high officials exercise authority over them. 26 Not so with you. Instead, whoever wants to become great among you must be your servant, 27 and whoever wants to be first must be your slave— 28 just as the Son of Man did not come to be served, but to serve, and to give his life as a ransom for many."
—**Matthew 20:20-21, 24-28**

For we are God's workmanship, created in Christ Jesus to do good works, which God prepared in advance for us to do.
—**Ephesians 2:10**

Faith by itself, if it is not accompanied by action, is dead. … 18 But someone will say, 21 Was not our ancestor Abraham considered righteous for what he did when he offered his son Isaac on the altar? 22 You see that his faith and his actions were working together, and his faith was made complete by what he did. 23 And the scripture was fulfilled that says, "Abraham believed God, and it was credited to him as righteousness," and he was called God's friend. 24 You see that a person is justified by what he does and not by faith alone.
—**James 2:17, 21-24**

19

Then the mother of Zebedee's sons came to Jesus with her sons and, kneeling down, asked a favor of him. 21 "What is it you want?" he asked. She said, "Grant that one of these two sons of mine may sit at your right and the other at your left in your kingdom."… 24 When the ten heard about this, they were indignant with the two brothers. 25 Jesus called them together and said, "You know that the rulers of the Gentiles lord it over them, and their high officials exercise authority over them. 26 Not so with you. Instead, whoever wants to become great among you must be your servant, 27 and whoever wants to be first must be your slave— 28 just as the Son of Man did not come to be served, but to serve, and to give his life as a ransom for many."
—Matthew 20:20-21, 24-28

For we are God's workmanship, created in Christ Jesus to do good works, which God prepared in advance for us to do.
—Ephesians 2:10

Faith by itself, if it is not accompanied by action, is dead. … 18 But someone will say, 21 Was not our ancestor Abraham considered righteous for what he did when he offered his son Isaac on the altar? 22 You see that his faith and his actions were working together, and his faith was made complete by what he did. 23 And the scripture was fulfilled that says, "Abraham believed God, and it was credited to him as righteousness," and he was called God's friend. 24 You see that a person is justified by what he does and not by faith alone.
—James 2:17,21-24

20

THE BUSINESS PLAN

You and your group are <u>business partners,</u> and planning a <u>restaurant</u> venture <u>investing</u> mega-bucks to provide an exceptional <u>product</u> and generate maxi-<u>profit</u>. The plan includes <u>job descriptions,</u> and <u>employees</u> will be selected with <u>abilities</u> to do their jobs well. Generous <u>bonuses</u> will be given to those who faithfully do their jobs.

YOUR TASK (Part 1): Brainstorm and list four vital jobs and the abilities each will require.

	Job	Required Abilities
Sue	_____	_____
Joe	_____	_____
Helen	_____	_____
Bob	_____	_____

YOUR TASK (Part 2): Discuss—

• *What would happen if these people do not do their jobs? What things might keep them from performing? How would you solve these problems?*

FIGHTING OVER THE PRESENTS?

Have you ever seen siblings quarreling over Christmas presents? "My gift is better than your gift!" one taunts.

"Is not! Mine's better!" the other blares in return. Soon, rather than enjoying their presents, they are at war.

"Now about spiritual gifts, I do not want you to be ignorant," Paul wrote to some Christians who were acting like children. Rather than experiencing the joy of using their gifts for the purposes God had intended, they were arguing over whose gift was best. Sadly, the same arguments still arise today.

Instructions: Develop fictional examples of "real-life" kinds of gifts-in-conflict stories in the church. Then work on practical solution suggestions:

Story 1:

Story 2:

Story 3:

It's vital that we know what spiritual gifts do, who receives them, and how the different gifts work together. Christians can't afford to be at war with one another. Our brothers and sisters in Christ are not the enemy!

Take Home Page

THE NEXT STEP
Projects and Ideas for the Week Ahead

•**Single Parents.** Assign chores to your children that they are capable of doing well. Explain how important their tasks are, and how they will help you accomplish all that you have to do. When they have finished, thank them for a job well done. Reward them by sharing an activity they enjoy. As you spend time together, explain to them that God created them with special abilities and that He has special purpose for them. Name and affirm their abilities. Explain that just as you have rewarded them for doing something you knew they could do well, God rewards His children when we do what He has designed us to do.

•**Group Repair Project.** Look around your church, neighborhood, or a worthwhile nonprofit organization that has a building needing painting, roofing, or other repairs. Locate available funding resources for materials; seek wholesale sources or contributions from local vendors. Volunteer as a group to provide labor. Have one or two good recruiters contact their classmates and solicit their participation. Those who are unable by physical or skill limitations to do the labor can provide food and drinks for those who are working. Plan a celebration party when the work is completed.

A GROUP PRAYER FROM 1 PETER . . .

"Above all, love each other deeply, because love covers over a multitude of sins. Offer hospitality to one another without grumbling. Each one should use whatever gift he has received to serve others, faithfully administering God's grace in its various forms. If anyone speaks, he should do it as one speaking the very words of God. If anyone serves, he should do it with the strength God provides, so that in all things God may be praised through Jesus Christ. To him be the glory and the power for ever and ever. Amen" (1 Peter 4:8-11).

Pray individually, with a friend, or taking turns in your group, that the single adults in your circle of friends will be able to apply each statement in the passage above: that you will grow to love each other deeply, be hospitable toward each other without grumbling, use your gifts to serve others, etc. Don't forget to give glory to God for His provision of Christian friendships!

SHAPE UP!

Over the course of this study, we will look at how God forms each of us with unique combinations of attributes, which form our "SHAPE" for service. Can you fill in the blanks?

S _____ **Gifts**
The "what" we do in ministry. (Session 2)

H _____ **'s Desires**
The "where" we do our ministry. (Session 4)

A _____
Our physical, mental, emotional resources. (Session 4)

P _____ **Style**
Our unique way of being and relating. (Session 5)

_____
How God instructs, guides, and matures us. (Session 6)

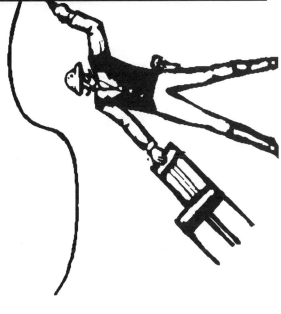

IN OTHER WORDS...

Vocation: It comes from the Latin vocare, to call, and means the work a person is called to by God. There are all different kinds of voices calling you to all different kinds of work, and the problem is to find out which is the voice of God rather than of Society, say, or the Superego, or Self-Interest.

By and large a good rule for finding out is this: The kind of work God usually calls you to is the kind of work (a) that you need most to do and (b) that the world most needs to have done.

If you really get a kick out of your work, you've presumably met requirement (a), but if your work is writing cigarette ads, the chances are you've missed requirement (b). On the other hand, if

(CONTINUES FLIPSIDE)

Take Home Page

continued

DAILY READINGS AND REFLECTIONS

This week's study focused on just a few Scriptures. Here are some additional Bible passages you may enjoy reading—about how and why God prepares us for service.

Monday: Read Mark 10:42-45. Jesus tells His disciples how to become great.

Tuesday: Read I Peter 4:10-11. Peter teaches about faithfulness in serving.

Wednesday: Read James 2:14-26. Authentic faith demands action!

Thursday: Read Psalm 139:13-16. Before we are born, God has a plan for us.

Friday: Read Colossians 3:23-24. The Lord rewards the work we do.

Saturday: Read Matthew 25:31-46. We will be judged according to our service.

Prayer: Lord, thank You for loving me and designing me with purpose. I want to become more aware of the abilities You have given me. I want to experience the joy of serving in the unique way You've designed me to serve. Teach me Your ways, Lord, and increase my understanding. Amen.

BRING THE LESSON HOME

• What are some of my fears about investing the spiritual, mental, physical, emotional, and material resources God has given me?

• Do I really believe that God has created me with purpose? How would my life change if I had a better understanding of what He has designed me to do?

• Single parents: When I was the age that my children are now, did I know that God created me with purpose? If I had known, how might my life be different today?

• In what ways could I develop a deeper understanding of God's design on my life, and help my children understand how He has designed them?

THINK—for Next Week: What are my spiritual gifts?

IN OTHER WORDS...

your work is being a doctor in a leper colony, you have probably met requirement (b), but if most of the time you're bored and depressed by it, the chances are you have not only bypassed (a), but probably aren't helping your patients much either.

Neither the hair shirt not the soft birth will do. The place God calls you to is the place where your deep gladness and the world's deep hunger meet.

—Frederick Buechner, *Wishful Thinking*

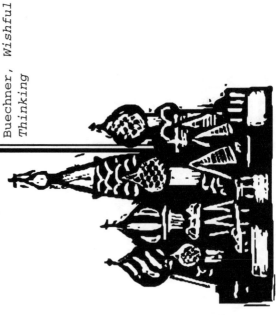

Session 2

TURN ON THE Power

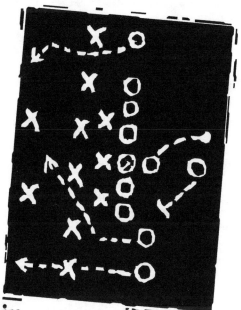

'Christianity has become nothing but a spectator sport, very much akin to the definition of football—22 men down on the field, desperately in need of rest, and 20 thousand in the grandstands, desperately in need of exercise!'*

Someone has said that the Holy Spirit could withdraw completely from many churches and their programs would continue without interruption. God never intended it to be so. The Holy Spirit transformed the disciples from fearful, ordinary men into bold, dynamic messengers. They joyfully went forth to do what Jesus had told them to do. They did it by exercising their spiritual gifts.

Spiritual gifts transcend natural abilities or talents. They are an energized link, spirit-to-Spirit, with God. He manifests His power through our gifts. He allows us to see through His eyes. Every one of us is given gifts to enable us to do our part in the dynamic work of the church on earth.

Single adults need to know that the dynamic power of the Holy Spirit is still available to believers today. He still transforms the mundane into the extraordinary. We simply need to turn on the Power!

*Ray C. Stedman, *Body Life* (Glendale, CA: Regal Books, 1972).

SESSION AIM

To help single adults develop a basic understanding of the functions and purposes of spiritual gifts

WHAT'S IT ALL ABOUT?

As you move through your session, keep in mind these Key Concepts you'll be conveying to your group members:

• Christians form the Body of Christ here on earth.
• God gives us various spiritual gifts to use in serving one another in the Body.
• Each gift is important and works together with all the others.
• Using our gifts helps us to grow mature in our faith.
• Using our gifts without love is worthless.

BIBLE REFERENCES:

Romans 12:4-6a
1 Corinthians 12:7, 24-27
Ephesians 4:11-16
1 Corinthians 13:1-3

23

HINT:

For "Cute Babies," have an extra word-set or two available to add, in case more people attend than expected.

HINT:

Optional Recording Idea.

Obtain a copy of Amy Grant's recording "Fat Babies." Arrange in advance for a trio from your group to put on a bib and lip-sync the song during your "Wrap It Up" time. Restate Key Concept 4 and announce that next week you'll get more specific about identifying nine spiritual gifts that drive us to minister in certain ways.

1—Let's Get Started
(5-10 minutes)

Option 1: Cute Babies
Needed: Interactive Page #1.

Identify how many people will be attending and how many groups you will need. Select "cute baby actions" to match the number of groups you want to have. For example, if you want five groups of four people, select the five actions of yawning, cooing, stretching, sucking a thumb, and shaking a rattle. Then make four slips of paper for each word you have selected. Place the paper slips in a container and have each person draw one.

Explain that participants are to portray the cute baby actions until everyone has found those who are doing the same action. Then, hand out Interactive Page #1 and invite discussion of the questions under "Cute Babies."

Option 2: Sentence Completion
Needed: Chalkboard and chalk.

Place the following on the chalkboard:

"When it comes to talent, I'd have to say I'm ..."

After fielding some responses, ask everyone to describe the difference—as they understand it— between "natural abilities" and "spiritual gifts." Be prepared to offer some definitions before moving into your biblical presentation.

2—Looking to the Word
(15 minutes)

1. Explain that God wants us to grow up to be spiritually mature, just as we grow up physically, mentally, and emotionally. He gives us spiritual gifts as a link with Him, spirit-to-Spirit, to lead us into specific kinds of service. As we use those gifts in serving each other, we become spiritually mature—individually and as a body of believers.

2. Refer to "What the Bible Has to Say" on page 28-30, and present the five key concepts, adding your own personal illustrations and subpoints, as appropriate.

3. If time permits, cover the "Going Deeper" explanations about church history regarding the Pentecostal, Charismatic, and Third Wave movements. This information will be especially helpful in groups with multiple denominational backgrounds.

3—Applying It to My Life
(5-10 minutes)

Needed: Interactive Page #1.

As soon as you complete your presentation, direct attention to "More Food for Thought" on Interactive Page #1. In groups of four to five, ask participants to discuss what happens when Christians don't grow up spiritually.

4—Taking the Next Step
(5 minutes)

In different groups of three to four, ask participants to describe one area of ministry that they seem drawn to which is either *especially good* or *especially faulty* in churches where they have attended. Ask them to reflect upon how their observation may relate to their giftedness.

After brief small group discussion, call for a sharing of insights.

5—Let's Wrap It Up
(5 minutes)

Needed: Take Home Page, "Defining the Gifts" handout.

1. Make your group's announcements at this time.

2. Distribute the Take Home Page and provide multiple copies of the handout titled "Defining the Gifts" on pages 31-32. Ask group members to read over the definitions of the gifts during the coming week and to seek affirmation of their potential gifts from at least two people who know them well.

3. Pray for the class to grow toward maturity—both individually and as a group—through each person's discovering and using his or her gifts.

When You Have More Time...
(How to Use This Material in 60-90 Minutes)
Example: Small Groups at Home

1—Let's Get Started
(5-10 minutes)

Option 1: Special Equipment
Needed: Interactive Page #2.

Direct attention to "Special Equipment" on Interactive Page #2 and discuss the special equipment required by your group members' favorite sports, hobbies, or activities. Invite stories about peoples' most outlandish true or imagined scenario of equipment malfunction.

In small groups, have people vote among themselves on the most outlandish equipment failure and share the winner's story with everyone. Select the grand-prize best story by applause vote. If time permits, have the groups guess whether the other groups' most outlandish story is truth or fiction.

Option 2: 'Word Descriptions'
Ask: "If you had to use only four words to state your 'job description' (what you do in life, whether formally employed or not), what four words would you use?"
Invite students to tell how they would describe their "calling" in life with just four words. Then discuss:

•*To what extent would you say you are "qualified" for the job you do?*
•*What is the nature of "spiritual qualifications" when attempting ministry work? How qualified are you, personally, in this area? Explain.*

2—Looking to the Word
(20-25 minutes)

1. Point out that spiritual gifts are "special equipment" to be used for ministry. Unlike manmade equipment, the gifts don't break down—but operator error can still have disastrous results! That's why Paul said, "Now, about spiritual gifts, I do not want you to be ignorant."
2. Present the material found in "Presenting What the Bible Has to Say," on pages 28-30.

3—Applying It to My Life
(20-25 minutes)

Needed: "Defining the Gifts" Handout; Interactive Page #2.

Once you complete your presentation, distribute the handout titled "Defining the Gifts," on pages 31 and 32 to small groups. Also refer the groups to Interactive Page #2's "More Food for Thought." Have each person select one of the gifts marked with an asterisk. Ask them to reflect on and discuss the "Food for Thought" question:

•*What could happen if the person who had that gift didn't use it?*

After a few minutes, have participants discuss their conclusions with their group.

4—Taking the Next Step
(10-20 minutes)

Ask everyone to recall the "Gift Snapshot" exercise in your mini-lecture. Have people take out their mental cameras once more. Ask:

•*If you were to take a snapshot of an area of ministry most interesting to you, what would appear in the photograph?*

Ask everyone to share with their group what their snapshot contains and why. Point out that this exercise may give a clue to the gifts they've been given for ministry.

5—Let's Wrap It Up
(5 minutes)

Needed: Take Home Page, "Defining the Gifts".

1. Make your group's announcements.
2. Distribute the Take Home Page and refer group members once again to the "Defining the Gifts" handout. Ask them to read over the definitions of the gifts during the coming week and to seek affirmation of their likely gifts by at least two people who know them well.
3. Ask a volunteer to close with a prayer that each person will develop a hunger to know and use his or her spiritual gifts.

HINT:

For Option 1 pick up a gag gift—in at least acceptably good taste, of course—to be awarded as a "worst equipment failure" prize.

HINT:

A "Closing Shot" Activity. For an optional closing activity, bring a camera. Divide the room into sections and direct each person to take a picture of a particular section. Relate the sections to the part the Holy Spirit would have them to do at your church (or other ministry). Announce that next week you will see how well their shots fit together to complete a picture of the room.

HINT:

Remember to plan plenty of interaction time in your small group setting. Watch for potential leaders and begin early to evoke their leadership gifts and potential.

HINT:

The video clips were carefully chosen to side-step PG-13 expletives that some of your singles might use if they were about to be swept up in a tornado!

HINT:

As you prepare for this session, pray for a deeper personal understanding of the gifts of the Spirit. Imagine what could occur in your group of singles if each began to use his or her gifts! Unless your singles are totally perfect, dream about resolving conflicts through using gifts in love. (If your singles are totally-perfect, of course, they already are just loving everything about each other—scripturally, of course!)

1—Let's Get Started
(20-30 minutes)

Option 1: "Twister"
Needed: Video rental.

Rent a video of the movie "Twister," and mark your starting points for the following clips: (1) Play a four-minute clip from the beginning, starting with the billboard, "June 1969," through the billboard, "Present Day."

While an assistant fast-forwards, explain that the little girl (Helen Hunt) grows up with a goal of finding a way to forecast tornadoes more accurately. She and her former husband (Bill Paxton) have developed a tracking device with electronic spheres which, when swept up in the twister, should transmit research data. Now, they must plant the machine in the tornado's path—and then split!

(2) The spheres are caught up by the storm. Start at this point and run for about four additional minutes, to the point where Paxton and Hunt get into the shed. Now form groups of four to five to discuss:

●*We can't see wind. How do we know it is there? What good and what harmful things does wind do?*
●*How is the Holy Spirit like wind?*

Have the groups report their findings.

Option 2: What's in Your Lens?
Form small groups. Vividly describe a favorite outdoor panorama. Ask group members to imagine what they would photograph in that setting, then share what is in their lens and why. Explain that just as we each have favorite parts in a landscape, *the Holy Spirit focuses us on particular aspects of ministry.*

2—Looking to the Word
(20 minutes)

1. Explain that today we begin a two-part study of a force much like wind. We can't see spiritual gifts, but we can observe their effects.

2. Teach from "What the Bible Has to Say," pages 28-30.

3—Applying It to My Life
(30-40 minutes)

Have everyone form small groups. Distribute blank index cards. Ask students to write their favorite hobby on the card, then pass it to their right. Then, ask each to say,

"I love to _____ (name the hobby from the card they received). I do it by _____ (describe procedures for their own activity)."

Other group members must guess what activity the reader is actually describing. Then explain that our gifts do not fit some jobs. By observation, we can help each other identify our potential gifts. As we serve, we discover whether our gifts were correctly named.

4—Taking the Next Step
(30-40 minutes)

Needed: "Defining the Gifts" Handout.

Distribute "Defining the Gifts," from pages 31 and 32. Read aloud from the handout: "Remember that the task of the church is three-fold:..." and have participants read the three tasks aloud with you. Ask them to reflect for a moment and then share with a partner:

●*If you were to invest your energies in just one of those three tasks, which would you choose—and why?*

After 10-12 minutes, form small groups of those who chose the same task. Ask everyone to scan the gifts under their chosen task and share if any of the gifts describe them or are of particular interest.

5—Let's Wrap It Up
(5 minutes)

Make your group's announcements. Distribute the Take Home Page and additional "Defining the Gifts" copies. Ask group members to do "Bringing the Lesson Home" during the coming week and to seek affirmation of their potential gifts from at least two people who know them.

My Personal Game Plan

STEP 1   Time: _____ minutes.

Materials Needed:

Activities Summary:

STEP 2   Time: _____ minutes.

Materials Needed:

Activities Summary:

STEP 3   Time: _____ minutes.

Materials Needed:

Activities Summary:

STEP 4   Time: _____ minutes.

Materials Needed:

Activities Summary:

STEP 5   Time: _____ minutes.

Materials Needed:

Activities Summary:

Just for You
Teacher's Devotional

What impact will this series have on your ministry leadership? Let me suggest two things for your focus as you proceed through this course. Each point has an excellent quotation to go with it—statements you may wish to jot in your journal, as I have. First, *develop the art of recognizing the gifts in your students*. Elbert Hubbard said, "There is something that is much more scarce, something finer far, something rarer than ability. It is the ability to recognize ability."*

Second, *commit to developing your own gifts and using them effectively*. "All great leaders have understood that their number one responsibility was for their own discipline and personal growth," states John Maxwell. "If they could not lead themselves, they could not lead others. Leaders can never take others farther than they have gone themselves, for no one can travel without until he or she has first traveled within."+ What are your gifts? How do your gifts shape how you minister to your class? Seek a deeper understanding of your own giftedness. Are you using your gifts in love?

As you learn more about how the gifts are functioning in your own life, you'll be more likely to see and appreciate how they work in the lives of your students, too. It's a potent combination! And this approach will move your entire group closer to the biblical ideal of mutual edification and effective outreach—all through the power of the Holy Spirit.

—Lana Wilkinson

*Elbert Hubbard, in Alan Loy McGinnis, *Bringing Out the Best in People* (Minneapolis: Augsburg Publishing House, 1985).

+John C. Maxwell, *Developing the Leader Within You* (Nashville: Thomas Nelson Publishers, 1993).

MY GOALS FOR THIS SESSION:

- TO HELP SINGLE ADULTS
_____
_____
_____

- TO HELP SINGLE ADULTS
_____
_____
_____

- TO HELP SINGLE ADULTS
_____
_____
_____

- TO HELP SINGLE ADULTS
_____
_____
_____

WHAT I LEARNED FROM READING 'LOOKING TO THE WORD' . . .

Notes and Insights—

27

LOOKING TO THE WORD—TURN ON THE POWER!

Presenting
What the Bible Has to Say...

Here's your mini-lecture covering the biblical Key Concepts. Try to become familiar with the flow of thoughts, and the outline, in order to present this material with maximum eye contact. Special instructions to you are in bold type. (Note: Have group members refer to the Key Concepts section on their Interactive Page. They may wish to fill in the blanks as you speak.)

Introduction

Illustration: A Snapshot in Your Mind. Begin by having everyone close their eyes and visualize their favorite outdoor scene. Then imagine selecting a particular shot for a photo. Will it be a wide angle? A focus on a particular flower? A picture of an animal or bird? You may want to ask people to describe their visions and tell what they framed in their snapshot—and why they made that particular choice.

Optional: Second, explain recent church history in relation to the Pentecostal, Charismatic, and Third Wave movements. This information is especially helpful in groups with multiple denominational backgrounds (see "Going Deeper").

Someone has said that the Holy Spirit could withdraw completely from many of our churches and their programs would continue without interruption. Is it true? Has Christianity simply become a spectator sport, with the "professionals" fighting it out on the playing fields and the rest of us looking on, offering the occasional cheer? Or are we all called to be involved in the Kingdom battles?

THE KEY CONCEPTS

We know that the Holy Spirit transformed the disciples from fearful, ordinary people into bold, dynamic messengers. They joyfully went forth to do what Jesus had told them to do. They did it through the power of their spiritual gifts.

Transition Statement: But how much do we really know about the gifts of the Spirit? Let's get an overview of five key statements about the nature of these gifts...

Read 1 Corinthians 12:31 aloud.

From this Scripture verse we can learn our first Key Concept about building community—

KEY CONCEPT #1:
Christians form the Body of Christ here on earth.

Read aloud Romans 12:4-5.

When Jesus ascended, He instructed His disciples to be His witnesses, to make more disciples, and to teach them to obey the things He had commanded. Christians today carry on that work.

Illustration. Did you read about the little boy who returned home after his first Sunday school class? His mother asked, "Who was your teacher?" The little boy answered, "I don't remember her name, but she must have been Jesus' grandmother, because she didn't talk about anyone else."

•*Think: In what ways is it clear to those who know you that you are a member of Christ's Body—His family on earth?*

KEY CONCEPT #2:
God gives us various spiritual gifts to use in serving one another in the Body.

Read aloud 1 Corinthians 12:7.

We studied last week that we are to serve each other. Jesus told His disciples to wait for the Holy Spirit before beginning to be His witnesses. He didn't send them to do His work with just their own abilities, but

in the power of the Spirit.

This course shouldn't be a sterile study of theory and theology. It is a look at the dynamic, life-changing power of the Holy Spirit working in and through believers today. Do not simply learn about spiritual gifts. Experience the Holy Spirit in action through *using your gifts!* When you experience His power, your life and the lives you touch are transformed.

- *When have your spiritual gifts been in full operation?*
- *Will a person necessarily know it when functioning in the power of the Spirit?*

KEY CONCEPT #3:
Each gift is important and works together with all the others.

According to 1 Corinthians 12:24-27, God created us to be interdependent.

Object lesson. Quickly exchange left shoes with your partner! . . . Who is in pain? Does your foot hurt but the rest of you feel great? What insights can you draw from this little exercise?

The point: For a quick demonstration of the importance of our parts working together, think about how your whole body suffers when your shoes are too tight!

KEY CONCEPT #4:
Using our gifts helps us to grow mature in our faith.

Read aloud Ephesians 4:11-16.

We might relate all of this to playing football. We can read all the rule books. We can play the video games and play Monday morning quarterback. But we grow in our ability to play the game only as we practice with the team and work up a sweat against the competition. Likewise, there is an element of spiritual growth that occurs only as we *use* our gifts in serving one another. In a sense, we've got to keep trying out ministries to get the right "fit"!

Illustration. We can develop our gifts. A reporter once said to George Bernard Shaw: "You have a marvelous gift for oratory. How did you develop it?" Shaw retorted, "I

learned to speak as people learn to skate or cycle, by doggedly making a fool of myself until I got used to it."

In trying out our gifts in ministry, we won't be making fools of ourselves, but we will no doubt make mistakes. This is all a part of the learning and maturing process.

KEY CONCEPT #5:
Using our gifts without love is worthless.

Read aloud 1 Corinthians 13.

Lack of love caused the quarrels Paul addresses in 1 Corinthians 12. When Paul wrote the "Love Chapter," 1 Corinthians 13, he was not writing a wedding sermon! He was writing to Christians who were arguing over petty things, including who was more spiritual than whom in the use of which gift. Paul emphatically states that our "love quotient" is the final test of the proper use of our gifts! We can live a pious life—and live it all to ourselves, never reaching out in love. That is truly a sad existence.

Conclusion

Illustration: Another Snapshot. Once again, close your eyes and recall your favorite outdoor setting. Perhaps you are enjoying ocean breezes from your lounge chair on a sunny summer day; waves are crashing on the rocks and gulls cry overhead. Or it's fall in the Rockies and the crisp air energizes you; you spy a waterfall bursting over a cliff ringed by shimmering aspens and stately evergreens. Maybe it's spring in the hill country; you catch your breath as you discover a field of bluebonnets and Indian paintbrush around a weathered old farmhouse and windmill. Paint the picture in your mind. Bask in it.

Now, imagine that this scene represents all the tasks God wants done by the body of believers where you worship. Each person is to photograph a particular part of the scene. God gives each person a camera and shows him or her where to focus. Each camera has a particular lens, filter, depth, and breadth of field. Some focus on minute detail; others see a broader picture. Some picture the clouds; others, the lay of the land. All the photographs will fit together to complete the panoramic view.

Spiritual gifts work much like those cameras. God determines which part of the picture we see. Some of us minister to one set of needs while others do something

HINT:

Teach with an open Bible, rather than reading Scriptures from a study guide or some other source. Also, be sensitive to those who may be uncomfortable reading or praying aloud. Never take turns reading or praying around the room; don't just call on someone to pray unless you know their comfort level.

of needs while others do something entirely different. Often, we are unable to comprehend the part that God has gifted someone else to do. In other words, we tend to view ministry through the spiritual eyes of our God-given gifts.

Say "Yes!" with purpose! The Holy Spirit urges us to take action upon what He enables us to see. We are never content until we answer "Yes" to His call. Through our spiritual gifts, God directs, energizes, and empowers us to accomplish His work for His purposes.

GOING DEEPER

"Gifts" in the Greek. The translation "spiritual gifts" does not do justice to the meaning of the original language. There are actually three Greek words translated "spiritual gifts": *pneumatikons* (1 Cor. 12:1)—that which pertains to the spirit (spiritual things); *charismaton* (2 Cor. 12:4)—performance accomplished through the energy given by God; *phanerosis* (1 Cor. 12:7)—making visible, shining forth, making known, manifestation.

Thus the gifts transcend natural abilities or talents. They are "spiritual things"—works performed by God's energy, which (when used properly) shine forth the very presence of God.

The "Love Chapter" in Context. In 1 Corinthians 13 Paul's bottom-line teaching is that when we use the gifts without love, we've missed the whole point. Sometimes, however, our churches still act like kids fighting over presents. Consider some 20th-century church history—

The Pentecostal Movement. At the beginning of the 20th century, the Pentecostal movement burst forth. Signs, wonders, and other miraculous ministries were outwardly characteristic of first- and early second-generation Pentecostals. Traditional Christians wrote the movement off as misguided theology. The disagreement over the miraculous gifts created two basic camps: Evangelicals and Pentecostals.

One belief common to conservative Evangelicals and others is known as cessationalism. It holds that "manifestation" gifts such as healing, speaking in or interpreting tongues, and miracles were present only to establish the authority of Jesus and the apostles prior to the completion of Scripture. When the canon of Scripture was complete, such gifts ceased. Evidence of manifestation gifts was often viewed as false at best and demonic at worst. Some evangelical seminaries train their students from this viewpoint.

Charismatic Renewal. In the early 1960s, a charismatic renewal began. Spiritual manifestations common to the early Pentecostal movement began to occur among denominations such as Lutherans, Episcopalians, and Roman Catholics. As a result, many church splits occurred during the 1960s and 1970s between Charismatics, who practiced signs and wonders, and traditional Evangelicals, who did not. One thought-provoking book, *Body Life,* written by Ray Stedman in the early 1970s, presented to traditional evangelical believers the need to involve all members of the Body—not just paid church staff—in using their spiritual gifts to advance the kingdom of God.

In the following decades, thoughtful Christians have worked at resolving these differences. During the late 1970s John Wimber, a professor at Fuller Theological Seminary, started a church where miraculous healings began to occur. The principles he began teaching at Fuller sparked great controversy and eventually resulted in modification of the seminary's position regarding the gifts of the Spirit.

The Third Wave. Today, a movement known as the "third wave" has produced increasing numbers of biblical scholars, theologians, and pastors who have examined the evidence on both sides of the issue. Those desiring additional information are encouraged to obtain Dr. Roger Barrier's 13-cassette Spiritual Gifts Series.* For reading on the "third wave," *The Kingdom and the Power,* published by Regal Books in 1993, edited by Gary S. Greig and Kevin N. Springer, contains chapters written by numerous evangelical leaders. Another recent, well-researched book is *Surprised by the Power of the Spirit* by Jack Deere (1993, Zondervan).

Whatever our position on the "signs and wonders" gifts may be, we all can agree upon the five primary concepts in this session. Let us focus on identifying our gifts in order to more effectively serve one another.

*Dr. Roger Barrier, "Spiritual Gifts Series" (tape series). Groupings and definitions of the gifts in this course are predominantly adapted from this series. Used by permission.

EXTRA INFORMATION TO CONSIDER...

Use this handout as your session leader suggests, or take it home with you for review during the week.

'DEFINING THE GIFTS'

What is a Spiritual gift? A spiritual gift is a spiritual manifestation of the Holy Spirit working through a believer's life to enable the Church to execute its task on earth. Spiritual gifts transcend natural abilities or talents. They are an energized link, spirit-to-Spirit, with God. He manifests His power through our gifts. He allows us to see through Holy Spirit eyes. Every Christian is given unique combinations of gifts to enable us to do our part in the work of the Church on earth.

Because the gifts are not defined in Scripture, they are subject to interpretation and resulting disagreement. Differences in interpretation include (1) whether all gifts still operate today, (2) whether other passages name attitudes, abilities, disciplines or gifts, and (3) precisely at what time gifts are received. Don't get hung up on areas where we may disagree. Attempt to identify your gifts and use them for God's purposes.

Remember that the task of the church is three-fold: To reach people, to mature Christians in Christ, and to organize the Church for effective ministry.

Gifts for Reaching People

Apostleship: A special leadership capacity in which one is sent cross-culturally to establish new works to enhance the spread of Christianity. It may be transcultural in that it reaches an unchurched subculture within our nation.

*Evangelism: The capacity to persuade people both publicly and privately with the Good News of salvation, so that people respond in conversion and in discipleship. It involves effective communication of the Gospel, as well as influencing Christians to evangelize.

Healing: The supernatural ability to heal people of physical disease in response to a laying on of hands, or praying, or commanding to be healed, or some combination of them by the person having the gift. [+] Healing is on the condition of the will of God, not the patient's faith.

*Mercy: A "beyond-the-average" capacity to empathize with those who are suffering and to show the sympathetic love of God by taking action to alleviate it with a cheerful spirit.

Miracles: An event of supernatural power, identifiable to the senses, accompanying a Christian, to authenticate the Word and/or the reality of God. Biblical miracles evidenced power over demons, nature, matter, disease and death. They occur most often in areas where the Gospel is just getting a foothold.

NOTE:

*Aterisks denote the "Driving Force" gifts.

[+]Dr. Robert Clinton, *Spiritual Gifts* (Canada: Horizon House, 1985), 82.

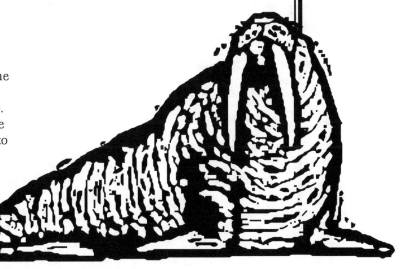

31

Gifts for Helping Christians Grow

Distinguishing Between Spirits (Discernment): The supernatural ability to differentiate between holy, human and demonic powers. This is not a natural ability to make wise decisions or a developed spiritual awareness. It is supernatural, God-given awareness of the operations of the spirit world.

*Exhortation (Encouragement): The spiritual capacity to: (1) urge people to action and to godly living and (2) encourage and comfort people through application of scriptural truths to their needs. It involves acceptance of another in his current condition, yet recognizing and stimulating growth toward his potential.

Faith: The Spirit-given ability to see something that God wants done and to believe that God will do it—regardless of seemingly insurmountable obstacles. It is visionary in its exercise, seeing beyond what others see, trusting and acting upon God's guidance and resources.

*Giving: The ability to give with joy and eagerness, without mixed motives for personal benefit. It is marked by zeal and sacrifice on the part of the giver, yet careful discrimination as to the recipients.

*Helps (Service): A special God-given gift for meeting the practical needs of people. It involves supporting another by taking her burden and placing it upon one's self. Its use is marked by an unassuming, less-talk-more-action style of serving others.

*Prophecy: The capacity to report a message from God to a particular situation in a current context. It involves revelation from the Holy Spirit and a report to others. It is manifested through "forthtelling" God's Word and will for the present and/or "foretelling" God's plans for the future.

*Teaching: The spiritual capacity to interpret, clarify, explain and preserve the truths of God. It involves not mere talent to impart information, but spiritually-energized, clear communication of concepts, which compels life-changing action.

Tongues: The ability to speak in a language unknown to the speaker. Biblically, tongues occur both as previously unlearned languages and as ecstatic utterances. Paul gave specific instructions in 1 Corinthians 14 regarding abuses of the gift.

Interpreting Tongues: The ability to understand and translate the language of one who is speaking in tongues. This is not interpreting a known language, but rather a revelation by the Holy Spirit of the meaning of the utterance. Its focus is communication of God-given ideas.

Word of Knowledge: A supernaturally-revealed communication of helpful knowledge for a current situation. It is not merely knowledge in general or a depth knowledge of Scripture. It depends upon sensitivity to the Holy Spirit for application to a specific situation.

Word of Wisdom: The supernatural capacity to synthesize concepts, facts and truths, to produce the needed God-inspired solution for a particular situation. This is not just wisdom in general which we all have from God. It is a "word" for a particular situation whose authority is recognized by others.

Gifts that Organize the Church for Effective Ministry

*Administration: The spiritual capacity to organize and manage the church. The person with the gift of administration instinctively understands and can develop the elements of structure necessary to support the task to be done.

Leadership: The spiritual capacity to attract people by creating a vision for the future and inspiring them to make the vision a reality. The gift involves dreaming about the future, being willing to risk changes, knowing which changes are worth the effort, and building teamwork by enlisting and inspiring others.

*Pastoring (Shepherding): The spiritual capacity to guide, guard and grow a group of people to be like Christ. It involves a long-term commitment to each person in a group—by example and by instruction—to love, guard, rescue, warn, protect, guide, heal, nourish and, when necessary, confront them as they grow.

HINT:

The "Gift Lists" in Scripture—

Romans 12:6-8

1 Corinthians 12:7-11

1 Corinthians 12:28

Ephesians 4:11-12

CUTE BABIES

Discuss with your group:

1. Name some things that make babies cute.
2. What are some things babies do that *aren't* so cute?
3. How would you respond if either of those characteristics were displayed by your boss at work? Your roommate? Your parents?

More Food for Thought— *on overgrown babies.* Without naming names, describe an adult Christian you have known who has failed to grow up spiritually. What evidences of immaturity have you observed? How did their behavior affect you or others around them?

KEY CONCEPTS
on the Spiritual Gifts

#1 Christians form the _____ __ _____ here on earth.

#2 God gives us various _____ _____ to use in serving one another in the Body.

#3 Each gift is _____ and works _____ with all the others.

#4 Using our gifts helps us to _____ _____ in our faith.

#5 Using our gifts without _____ is worthless.

MAKING BEAUTIFUL MUSIC TOGETHER

Imagine that the work God wants done in your church or community is a symphony orchestra. God is the conductor. Christians are the orchestra members. Spiritual gifts are the instruments. When everyone learns her part and follows the conductor, beautiful music flows forth. If we each "do our own thing" together, discord results. With that scenario in mind, read the statements below and check those that describe you.

___ I harmonize well with others (Sign me up for the symphony!)

___ I want to do a solo (Why practice, if you won't see me?)

___ I do my best, but miss some notes (I'm poor at watching the conductor.)

___ I usually sit in the audience (Just let me soak it in!)

___ I'm looking for my instrument (It was here somewhere; I've got to get organized!)

___ Other:_____

BIBLE TEXT

Just as each of us has one body with many members, and these members do not all have the same function, 5 so in Christ we who are many form one body, and each member belongs to all the others. 6 We have different gifts, according to the grace given us.
—Romans 12:4-6a

Now to each one the manifestation of the Spirit is given for the common good. … 24 while our presentable parts need no special treatment. But God has combined the members of the body and has given greater honor to the parts that lacked it, so that there should be no division in the body, but that its parts should have equal concern for each other. 26 If one part suffers, every part suffers with it; if one part is honored, every part rejoices with it. 27 Now you are the body of Christ, and each one of you is a part of it.
—1 Corinthians 12:7, 24-27

It was he who gave some to be apostles, some to be prophets, some to be evangelists, and some to be pastors and teachers, 12 to prepare God's people for works of service, so that the body of Christ may be built up 13 until we all reach unity in the faith and in the knowledge of the Son of God and become mature, attaining to the whole measure of the fullness of Christ. 14 Then we will no longer be infants, tossed back and forth by the waves, and blown here and there by every wind of teaching and by the cunning and craftiness of men in their deceitful scheming. 15 Instead, speaking the truth in love, we will in all things grow up into him who is the Head, that is, Christ. 16 From him the whole body, joined and held together by every supporting ligament, grows and builds itself up in love, as each part does its work.
—Ephesians 4:11-16

Just as each of us has one body with many members, and these members do not all have the same function, 5 so in Christ we who are many form one body, and each member belongs to all the others. 6 We have different gifts, according to the grace given us.
—Romans 12:4-6a

Now to each one the manifestation of the Spirit is given for the common good. … 24 while our presentable parts need no special treatment. But God has combined the members of the body and has given greater honor to the parts that lacked it, so that there should be no division in the body, but that its parts should have equal concern for each other. 26 If one part suffers, every part suffers with it; if one part is honored, every part rejoices with it. 27 Now you are the body of Christ, and each one of you is a part of it.
—1 Corinthians 12:7, 24-27

It was he who gave some to be apostles, some to be prophets, some to be evangelists, and some to be pastors and teachers, 12 to prepare God's people for works of service, so that the body of Christ may be built up 13 until we all reach unity in the faith and in the knowledge of the Son of God and become mature, attaining to the whole measure of the fullness of Christ. 14 Then we will no longer be infants, tossed back and forth by the waves, and blown here and there by every wind of teaching and by the cunning and craftiness of men in their deceitful scheming. 15 Instead, speaking the truth in love, we will in all things grow up into him who is the Head, that is, Christ. 16 From him the whole body, joined and held together by every supporting ligament, grows and builds itself up in love, as each part does its work.
—Ephesians 4:11-16

SPECIAL EQUIPMENT

1. Name a favorite sport, activity, or hobby that requires special equipment.
2. What equipment is required? Why is it needed?
3. Recall a true story or imagine a scenario about when the equipment didn't work properly. Try to outdo each other with outlandish results.

More Food for Thought—*on spiritual equipment.* Look at the "special equipment" listed on the "Defining the Gifts" handout. Choose a particular gift and describe a ministry function at your church that might require someone exercising that gift.

•*What could happen if the person who had that gift didn't use it? How can we "hook up" peoples' gifts with the needs in the church?*

KEY CONCEPTS
on the Spiritual Gifts

#1 Christians form the _____ __ _____ here on earth.

#2 God gives us various _____ _____ to use in serving one another in the body.

#3 Each gift is _____ and works _____ with all the others.

#4 Using our gifts helps us to _____ _____ in our faith.

#5 Using our gifts without _____ is worthless.

COULD YOU MAKE A DIFFERENCE?

Take some time this week to observe the needs around you. What do you notice that could be improved? Initiated? Communicated? Imagine what you, individually (or you and a group of your friends) might do to meet that need. In your journal, respond to the following:

I observed today that . . .

I think it needs to . . .

I—or my friends and I— could make a difference by . . .

Is this solution currently "do-able"? Why, or why not?

If it is "do-able," what would it take to do it?

Are training or resources needed? If so, where could I/we get them?

Who do I know that also might like to be involved?

What gifts and abilities do each of us bring to the table?

When can I/we get started?

Take Home Page

AFFIRMING YOUR GIFTS

Affirming the gifts of: _____

Date: _____ Completed by: _____
(Friend or Church Leader)

Refer to the descriptions in the "Defining the Gifts" handout and, based on your knowledge of this person, indicate below which of the listed gifts he or she may have. Use the following symbols:

+ any gift(s) you are definitely certain the person has

✓ any gift(s) you think may be one of this person's gifts

✗ any gift(s) you have actually observed him/her using effectively

✻ the "✻" (driving force) gift(s) you think may be this person's strongest

___ Apostleship

___ Prophecy*

___ Evangelism*

___ Teaching*

___ Healing

___ Tongues

___ Mercy*

___ Interpreting

___ Miracles

___ Tongues

___ Discernment

___ Word of Knowledge

___ Exhortation*

___ Word of Wisdom

___ Faith

___ Administration*

___ Giving*

___ Leadership

___ Helps*

___ Pastoring*

SHAPE UP!

Over the course of this study, we'er looking at how God forms each of us with unique combinations of attributes, which form our "SHAPE" for service. Can you fill in the blanks?

S _____ **Gifts**
The "what" we do in mi istry. (Session 2)

H _____'s **Desires**
The "where" we do our ministry. (Session 4)

A _____
Our physical, mental, emotional resouces. (Session 4)

P _____ **Style**
Our unique way of being and relating. (Session 5)

E _____
How God instructs, guides, and matures us. (Session 6)

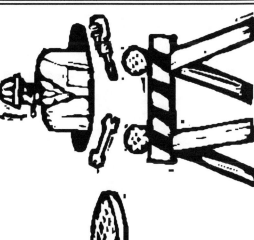

Take Home Page ABC continued

DAILY READINGS AND REFLECTIONS

This week's study focused on just a few Scriptures. Here are some additional passages you may enjoy reading about spiritual gifts.

Monday—Read 1Peter 4:7-11. Peter stresses vital attitudes when using our gifts.

Tuesday—Read Acts 1:4-8. Jesus tells the disciples to wait for the Holy Spirit's power and then to witness.

Wednesday—Read 1 Corinthians 13. Using our gifts without love is worthless.

Thursday—Read 1 Corinthians 2:9-16. Only Christians can receive the thoughts of God, i.e. spiritual gifts.

Friday—Read 1 Timothy 4:12-16. A youthful pastor is encouraged to persevere in using his spiritual gift.

Saturday—Read 1 Corinthians 12:21-25. All the parts of the Body need each other.

BRINGING THE LESSON HOME

Before studying "Defining the Gifts," answer theese two questions:

1. If you had no limitations (on time, finances, education, gender, etc.), what would you choose to do in Christian service?

2. I wish my church would be better at:

Retain your response for the balance of this study. It may help you identify your gift(s). Also, give a copy of "Defining the Gifts" to two or more people who know you well. Ask them to do the "Affirming Your Gifts" exercise.

If you have not been active in any area where someone can help to affirm your gifts, choose a place to serve and invest your energy there. Give the leader a copy of this handout and ask him/her to observe you over a period of time and give you feedback.

GETTING INTO ACTION

This week I will take the following deliberate action(s). Check all that apply:

___ Seek feedback on "Affirming Your Gifts"
___ Read the Daily Readings and Reflections
___ Journal which gift definitions seem to describe me
___ Ask God to reveal the gifts He's given me
___ Familiarize myself with the gift definitions
___ Observe what gifts others seem to possess
___ Commit to learning to use my gift(s)
___ Other:_____

THINK: For Next Week— Is it possible that the person at church who drives you totally crazy (and possibly vice versa) may just be ineffectively using his or her gift?

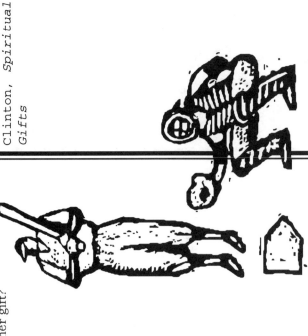

IN OTHER WORDS...

A quick survey of the major times of spiritual renewal in church history indicates that with each of these great movements there was a proliferation of small groups and a high degree of participation of lay individuals utilizing their basic talents, abilities or gifts. By recognizing and using our gifts we may see a great spiritual renewal in our day.

—Dr. James Robert Clinton, *Spiritual Gifts*

Session 3

Caution:
HIGH VOLTAGE!

Jesus told the apostles they'd receive power from the Holy Spirit to be His witnesses in their city, their territory, their neighboring territory, and ultimately the ends of the earth. That same power is available for the same purposes, today.

The Holy Spirit calls each of us to do certain kinds of works in the Body of Christ. He supernaturally equips us to do those works through our spiritual gifts. This is how the Good News is spread in every generation.

Your single adults need to know that every Christian—single or married, young or old—has a vital role to fulfill in community with other believers. There are nine gifts that we call "Driving Force Gifts" because they powerfully direct and propel the core of our individual ministries. Other gifts form a cluster with our Driving Force Gifts to provide a unique calling for each Christian.

The Holy Spirit urges us to do our part. Like parts of the human body, we are not created to stand alone. When we each understand our gifts, yield to the leadership of the Holy Spirit, and cooperate with one another, we become an awesome force for God's glory. Just as if we were plugged in to a high-voltage power source, ready to light up our world for Christ!

SESSION AIM

To help single adults recognize the Driving Force gifts and explore the uniqueness of their gift clusters.

WHAT'S IT ALL ABOUT?

As you move through your session, keep in mind these Key Concepts you'll be conveying to your group members:

•We receive power from the Holy Spirit for the purpose of spreading the Gospel.
•The Body of Christ is complete only when all its parts are working together.
•We each must understand our parts and how they work with the parts of others.

BIBLE REFERENCES:

Acts 1:8
Ephesians 4:1
1 Corinthians 12:14-25

Your 'Short Course' Set-Up...
(How to Use This Material in 35-45 Minutes)
Example: Sunday Morning Bible Study

HINT:

Use a combination of verbal, visual and hands-on exercises to appeal to each of the three modes of learning.

1—Let's Get Started
(5-10 minutes)

Option 1: Driving What, To Where?
Needed: Photocopies of popular vehicles, Interactive Page #1.

In advance, find pictures of several different types of popular vehicles and make four copies of each. Put together adequate numbers of sets of three for the group's normal attendance; shuffle and distribute as people arrive.

Ask everyone to form groups by matching pictures. Then distribute Interactive Page #1 and ask groups to write and then share their responses to "Driving What...To Where?"

Option 2: Right, Left, or Wrong Part?
Needed: Paper and crayons or markers.

Make available sheets of paper and an assortment of crayons or markers. Distribute paper and *one* color of crayon or marker per person. Give these instructions, allowing time for completion of each item before giving the next instruction:

1. Draw a simple, basic stick figure.
2. Use your other hand to draw the same figure.
3. Draw the figure by holding the crayon with your toes, elbow, or mouth.
4. Using your original hand, draw the figure in a different color.

Have everyone show his or her artwork to the groups and discuss how each instruction became more difficult and less effective, and eventually impossible—*unless they shared their resources.*

2—Looking to the Word
(15 minutes)

Teach the material on pages 42-45.

3—Applying It to My Life
(5-10 minutes)

Needed: Interactive Page #1.

1. If you used the first opener, refer participants back to their Interactive Page.

Ask them to read and respond to "Sharing your Prize," then to read "Think It Over." Re-form into previous buzz groups and ask everyone to discuss the importance of sharing the gifts they have been given.

2. If you used "Right, Left, or Wrong Part," reform the same groups. Ask everyone to use their normal writing hand and draw multiple-colored stick figures, sharing their colors both within their group and with neighboring groups. Ask people to compare these stick figures with the previous drawings. Then ask:

• *How does this exercise illustrate the importance of knowing what part of the Body of Christ we are—and of working together in ministry?*

Allow a few minutes for discussion.

4—Taking the Next Step
(5 minutes)

1. Distribute the handout titled "The Driving Force Gifts" on pages 45-46. Explain spiritual gifts in terms of colored lenses. Help the group visualize evangelism as the color red, with supporting gifts in their cluster blending to create various shades of red.

2. Point out the Driving Force Gifts descriptions and the "good-news/bad-news" characteristics of the gifts. Explain that we need to be aware not only of the focus of our gifts, but also of the potential misuses.

• *If you have observed this gift, was it used effectively or ineffectively? Why?*

5—Let's Wrap It Up
(5 minutes)

Needed: Take Home Page, "Defining the Gifts" Handout.

Distribute the Take Home Page and provide multiple copies of the handout titled "Defining the Gifts" on pages 31 and 32. Ask group members to read over the definitions of the gifts during the coming week and to seek affirmation of their potential gifts from at least two people who know them well.

When You Have More Time...
(How to Use This Material in 60-90 Minutes)
Example: Small Groups at Home

1—Let's Get Started
(5-10 minutes)

Option 1: This Describes Me Best
Needed: Interactive Page #2.

Direct attention to Interactive Page #2. Ask small groups to select their top one or two phrases from "This Describes Me Best" and share a recent example of how that description fit them well.

Option 2: Descriptions in Paperback
Needed: Blank sheets of paper, small bowl.

Give each person a piece of paper and have everyone anonymously write three to five characteristics that best describe him or her. Place the pieces of paper into a bowl and invite each member to take one and read it aloud. Have the group guess whose description is being read.

After some discussion, point out that today you'll be looking at nine "Driving Force Gifts." Just as we can guess a person's identity by their characteristics, we can recognize these gifts by their characteristics. We need to understand these gifts and how they work. They provide a Spirit-led focus for our ministries.

2—Looking to the Word
(20-25 minutes)

Present the material found in "Presenting What the Bible Has to Say," on pages 42-44.

3—Applying It to My Life
(20-25 minutes)

Needed: Gift-Cluster Handout, Interactive Page #2.

1. Once you complete your presentation, distribute the handout titled "The Driving Force Gifts" on pages 44-45. Touch briefly on the concept of gifts acting as colored lenses through which we view ministry. Stress that our Driving Force gift provides the primary "color" of our lenses and that our supporting gifts combine to give each person a unique "look" at ministry.

2. Refer to "What Drives You" on Interactive Page #2. Assist anyone who has difficulty matching the descriptions from Step 1 with the Driving Force Gifts. Ask groups to discuss whether the corresponding descriptions fit each person. If the descriptions fit well, they may provide a clue to the person's Driving Force gifts.

3. If time permits, ask everyone to read through the descriptions of the Driving Force gifts, to check each characteristic that fits them, and to determine which gift has the greater number of checks.

4. When everyone has finished, form groups to discuss: which gift(s) scored highest for each person, what characteristics they see in themselves, and whether they can affirm those characteristics for each other.

4—Taking the Next Step
(10-20 minutes)

Needed: Take Home Page.

Distribute the Take Home Page and invite everyone to complete the Driving Force Gifts Mini-Evaluation. When they have completed the quiz, have them compare the gift(s) they have chosen from the quiz and the gift(s) that emerged strongest in Step 3. Were they the same? Ask people to share their findings with a partner or small group.

Stress that the exercises and quizzes are simply tools to give clues to giftedness. Discovery and confirmation occur as people actually *use* their gifts

5—Let's Wrap It Up
(5 minutes)

Make your group's announcements and close in prayer.

HINT:

Use either Interactive Page #1 or Interactive Page #2 for a handout. Use any option from this page or from the previous Instruction Pages.

1—Let's Get Started
(20-30 minutes)

Option 1: My Favorite Activity

Form random groups and say: "Take turns describing and guessing your favorite sports or hobbies. In five words or less, tell what parts of your body are used and give information such as time of day, season of the year, indoors or out, with how many people, etc." When all have guessed the name of the hobby, ask each person to share why they enjoy the activity they have described.

Explain that this lesson examines our favorite ways to be involved in ministry—through our Driving Force Gifts. Quote Larry Gilbert: "Spiritual gifts are the 'want to' of Christian service."

Option 2: Discussion Questions

Begin your session with a free-flowing sharing time on the topic of "discovering your gifts." Start with questions like these:

  •*How do you respond to the idea that everyone should be involved in the ministry of the church?*
  •*To what extent is the "power" of the Holy Spirit something you can relate to? How do you know when this power is at work in your own life?*
  •*What is your most satisfying experience of working together with another person on a project? Of working with others in the church?*

2—Looking to the Word
(20 minutes)

Teach from pages 42-44, "Presenting What the Bible Has to Say."

3—Applying It to My Life
(30-40 minutes)

Needed: Handouts: "The Driving Force Gifts" and "Defining the Gifts" (extras from last week), a small container.

1. When you're through presenting "Looking to the Word," distribute the handout titled "the Driving force Gifts" on pages 45-46. Distribute last week's "Defining the Gifts" for any who missed last week or did not return with their definitions. Summarize the concept of gifts acting as colored lenses. Stress that our Driving Force Gift provides the primary "color" of our lenses and that our support gifts combine to give each person a unique "look" at ministry.

2. Now form three groups to play "charades" with the Driving Force gifts. (In advance, jot the nine gifts on slips of paper.) Give everyone time to ponder the nine gift descriptions. Then have each group select a person who will draw a gift and act out its characteristics.

Have each group take turns drawing and acting out two gifts. Allow a maximum of 60 seconds; time and record their scores. With the third gift, have all three groups draw their slips and wait for your signal to begin. Give a starting signal and record finish times for each group. Tally and announce the winning group.

4—Taking the Next Step
(30-40 minutes)

Needed: Take Home Page.

Hand out the Take Home Page and ask everyone to complete the Mini-Evaluation. Form groups of three to four to share the results and to discuss whether the descriptions of their apparent gift seem to fit them well. Discuss, for several of the group members' gifts:

  •*What general or specific jobs might be done by a person with this Driving Force Gift?*

5—Let's Wrap It Up
(5-10 minutes)

Make your group's announcements and then offer a prayer of thanksgiving for the group members and their gifts.

My Personal Game Plan

STEP 1   Time: _____ minutes.

Materials Needed:

Activities Summary:

STEP 2   Time: _____ minutes.

Materials Needed:

Activities Summary:

STEP 3   Time: _____ minutes.

Materials Needed:

Activities Summary:

STEP 4   Time: _____ minutes.

Materials Needed:

Activities Summary:

STEP 5   Time: _____ minutes.

Materials Needed:

Activities Summary:

Just for You
Teacher's Devotional

Whether or not you have time to teach all the information in these first three sessions, learn this material for yourself! Deeply soak in the definitions, characteristics, and "look-alike" gifts' differences. Comprehend fully your own gifts.

Jesus said: "Can a blind man lead a blind man? Will they not both fall into a pit? A student is not above his teacher, but everyone who is fully trained will be like his teacher. . . . The good man brings good things out of the good stored up in his heart, and the evil man brings evil things out of the evil stored up in his heart. For out of the overflow of his heart his mouth speaks" (Luke 6:39-40, 45).

What are you storing in your heart? After a period of silent meditation, make a little inventory list here:

-
-
-
-
-

What things are you happy to find in your heart? What things would it be good to remove? Are you ministering through the power of the Spirit or from your own personality and intellect? Spend time with the Lord. Allow Him to fill you so that His love overflows. Pray for discernment about your areas of self-sufficiency and for wisdom to rely more fully on Him.

—Lana Wilkinson

MY GOALS FOR THIS SESSION:

- TO HELP SINGLE ADULTS
_____
_____
_____

- TO HELP SINGLE ADULTS
_____
_____
_____

- TO HELP SINGLE ADULTS
_____
_____
_____

- TO HELP SINGLE ADULTS
_____
_____
_____

WHAT I LEARNED FROM READING 'LOOKING TO THE WORD' . . .

Notes and Insights—

41

LOOKING TO THE WORD—CAUTION: HIGH VOLTAGE!

Presenting What the Bible Has to Say...

Here's your mini-lecture covering the biblical Key Concepts. Try to become familiar with the flow of thoughts, and the outline, in order to present this material with maximum eye contact. Special instructions to you are in bold type. (Note: Have group members refer to the Key Concepts section on their Interactive Page. They may wish to fill in the blanks as you speak.)

Introduction

After His crucifixion, Jesus came back to life and appeared to His family and friends on a number of occasions. In one such gathering, He told the apostles that they would be His witnesses in their city, their territory, their neighboring territory and ultimately to the ends of the earth.

Ask a volunteer to read aloud Acts 1:8-9.

Now, think about this just a minute. These were the same guys, remember, who ran to save their hides when Jesus was crucified. Travel back and stand in the apostles' moccasins. Only forty days ago, your leader was strung up in public view. You feared that the same thing might happen to you. Just as you think it is all over, He comes back and hangs out with you. Now, He tells you that you're going to receive this extraordinary power and—by the way—you're going to tell the world about all these strange happenings. Before you can say, "I don't think so, Tim," He does this invisible elevator routine and disappears in the clouds.

•*What are you thinking and feeling as you look up in slack-jawed amazement?*

Ask for feedback on what your group members would have thought or felt under those circumstances. Help them experience the ambivalence of excitement and bewilderment, of fear and anticipation. Lead them to discover that nothing short of a supernatural power could have given these early

followers the necessary courage to risk ridicule, persecution, and death as they spoke and wrote about the events they had witnessed.

THE KEY CONCEPTS

Transition Statement: The words of Acts 1:8 are as relevant to believers today as they were to the apostles. We still are to be His witnesses. As we consider taking His message to the world, we experience many of the same doubts and fears. We still must rely on the Holy Spirit's power to do the job!

When we each understand our gifts, yield to the leadership of the Holy Spirit, and cooperate with one another, we are an awesome force for God's glory. Otherwise, we are either powerlessly ineffective or improperly divisive and destructive. That's why this session is called, "Caution: High Voltage!"

Let's consider three aspects of our calling and how it gets done most effectively:

•We receive power from the Holy Spirit for the purpose of spreading the Gospel.
•The Body of Christ is complete only when all its parts are working together.
•We each must understand our parts and how they work with the parts of others.

KEY CONCEPT #1: We receive power from the Holy Spirit for the purpose of spreading the Gospel.

We learn later in Acts that when the Holy Spirit appeared, these men boldly shared what they knew to be true. Three thousand people believed and were baptized. Not bad for Peter's first sermon!

Illustration. Let's relate the gifts of the Spirit to electricity and ourselves to electric appliances. Each appliance has specific work to do. It accomplishes that work effectively—when it is in good working order, is plugged in, and its switch is turned on. However, cut the power source and the appliance is unable to do its work.

If the appliance becomes defective, it does not work or may even be dangerous.

So it is with our gifts. We receive power from the Power Source, so that our gifts have the energy to operate—but we must turn on the switch. Our use of our gifts can be defective or divisive if we use them without love, without understanding, or with self-centered motives.

Ask a volunteer to read 1 Corinthians 12:14-21. Call for comments on what the passage means. After a few responses, make your transition to the next Key Concept:

Just as the parts of our physical bodies depend upon each other, our part in the Body of Christ depends upon all the other parts—which brings us to our next Key Concept.

KEY CONCEPT #2:
The Body of Christ is complete only when all its parts are working together.

Paul goes on to explain that like all the parts of our physical bodies, all the members of the church are important! Last week we saw that God has combined the parts in a way that each should have equal concern for the other. **Ask:**

•*What would happen if our brain signals got switched and our hands thought they were feet and vice versa?*

Encourage both funny and serious consequences. Think of some to share.

Optional object lesson. **Bring a pair (or if possible, several pair) of BluBlocker® sunglasses to class, along with several blue articles.**

Have you ever looked through colored lenses? If not, try it! Find some BluBlocker® sunglasses. Look through them at some blue articles. Does that change how you see shades of blue, or what?! Our spiritual gifts work much like colored lenses. God calls us to serve the needs He enables us to see. The Holy Spirit enables us to "see" our ministries through the "color" of our primary Driving Force gift. Our other gifts then combine with our Driving Force gift to produce our unique

ministry perspective—our gift cluster.

To illustrate, imagine that the Driving Force gift of evangelism is the color red. When the evangelist looks at the world, he or she sees it as red. Other gifts in the evangelist's cluster will blend to make one evangelist see burgundy while another sees tomato-red, but the basic color is still red.

We can relate the spectrum of spiritual gifts to the colors in a rainbow. Some are distinctly different; others look very similar and tend to merge into one another. All are necessary for the work to be complete.

KEY CONCEPT #3:
We each must understand our parts and how they work with the parts of others.

We have seen that the task of the church is three-fold: To reach people, to mature Christians in Christ and to organize the Church to reach more people and mature others. No one person has the ability, time nor energy to do all three tasks. Our Driving Force gifts predominantly determine which task(s) we are called to address. The support gifts will flavor how we approach the function of that ministry. It is important to begin to discover our predominate driving force, so that we can concentrate our efforts in that service.

A clue to identifying our Driving Force is that it will lead us into the work that is most energizing for us. Just when we think we are overdue for a rest, an opportunity to use our Driving Force gift will provide a new burst of wind beneath our wings. Conversely, serving for extended periods outside our primary areas of giftedness will result in apathy and frustration.

The Holy Spirit prompts us to do the work God has ordained for us to do. When we don't know our gifts, we may fail to recognize His calling. We are aware of the work that "somebody" should do—but we don't understand that the "somebody" who is to do the work is the person to whom God has revealed the need.

Conclusion

This week we want to look at nine gifts that we're calling "Driving Force Gifts." These gifts powerfully direct and propel the core of our individual ministries. We also want to understand how our "cluster" of gifts impacts how we use our Driving Force Gifts and provides unique direction.

GOING DEEPER

Look-Alike Gifts. Some of the gifts are like neighboring colors in a rainbow. They look a lot alike, but each has certain distinctive qualities. Let's examine some of these—

Administration and Helps. Both deal with organizing tasks. The administrator tends to comprehend over-all structure and long-term goals. He or she organizes in order to accomplish broad objectives, delegating responsibility when at all possible. The helper, on the other hand, is project and short-term oriented. He or she derives satisfaction from completing the work, rather than delegating it.

Teaching and Exhortation. Both communicate information for the purpose of maturing believers. Teachers tend to research Scripture for the sake of a broad base of knowledge, then relate that knowledge to life. Exhorters look at life's problems and turn to Scripture to find solutions. Teachers lean toward verse-by-verse Bible book studies; exhorters, toward topical, need-based studies.

Mercy and Helps. Both gifts work quietly behind the scenes. Mercy people minister to people's pain (both physical and emotional). Helps people deal with tasks that may meet a felt need, but their focus is on getting the job done—which ultimately ministers to the pain—rather than comforting the pain itself.

Exhortation, Mercy, and Prophecy. Exhortation looks a lot like a cross between mercy and prophecy. An exhorter will, for a reasonable time, comfort someone's pain. After that time, however, he or she will confront the person's need to take action to grow beyond, rather than wallow in, the problem.

Pastor/Shepherd, Administration, and Leadership. The driving force gifts of pastor/shepherd and administration both address the task of organizing the church. The pastor/shepherd deals with "herding the flock"—the people-related portion. The administrator takes care of the nuts-and-bolts task-oriented portion. A word of caution: Leadership is a support gift that may enhance any of the driving force gifts. It most often supports the people-oriented gifts of pastor/shepherd, exhortation and evangelism. Leadership is not the same as administration. Administrators rarely have the support gift of leadership. Leaders lead people; administrators focus on tasks. Leaders cast the vision; administrators implement it. Leaders influence people; administrators manage structure. Take care not to confuse the two.

Remember that our gifts are uncovered as we use them. They are affirmed in community with other believers. Blessings to you as you seek to effectively use your gifts to serve others for God's glory.

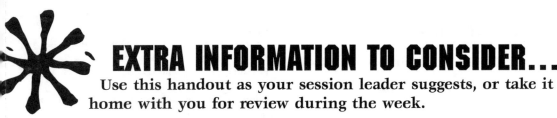

EXTRA INFORMATION TO CONSIDER...

Use this handout as your session leader suggests, or take it home with you for review during the week.

THE DRIVING FORCE GIFTS

By understanding the "good news / bad news" of each Driving Force gift, we can avoid personal pitfalls and lovingly help "babies" grow in their service. So, let's examine the Driving Force Gifts!

The Gift of Evangelism

Focus: Salvation of the Lost
Primary Misuse: Excessive Push for Decision; Insensitivity to People

Positive/Identifying Characteristics
Communicates the Gospel exceptionally well
Missions and outreach are given priority
Routinely turns normal conversations into discussions of eternal life
Studies Scripture to learn answers for each unbeliever's questions
Needs to see people take action and make decisions in response to sermons
Often active in secular pursuits in order to find witnessing opportunities

Misunderstandings/Misuses
Can confuse sense of worth with how many "notches on witnessing belt"
May become critical of others who are not actively involved in evangelism
Focus on salvation can ignore the person's physical or emotional needs
Danger of adopting non-Christian behavior to establish friendship with an unbeliever
May become more concerned with outward influence than private depth and integrity.

The Gift of Mercy

Focus: Alleviating Pain
Primary Misuse: Premature Rescue; Enabling Dysfunction

Positive/Identifying Characteristics
People with problems are drawn to them
Tears may flow when people are hurting
Values deep friendships, quality time, mutual commitment, physical closeness
Not easily repulsed by someone who is hurting; thinks, "How can I help?"
Avoids decisions and firmness unless they will alleviate hurt
Frequently friend of those with gift of prophecy

Misunderstandings/Misuses
Greater vulnerability to deep/frequent hurts
Sensitivity may encourage improper affections from the opposite sex
Appear to be guided by emotions, not logic
Tend to withdraw when hurt
May compromise principles to avoid conflict
Can be fooled by insincere cries for help

The Gift of Teaching

Focus: Educating; Increasing Knowledge
Primary Misuse: Overconfidence in Knowledge as the Ultimate Problem-Solver

Positive/Identifying Characteristics
Unsatisfied with unclear explanations offered by self or by others
Tests knowledge of those who teach
Avoids non-biblical sources and out-of-context Scriptural illustrations
Orientation goes from Scripture to experience
Alert to factual details not noticed by others
Frequently enjoys research more than presentation

Misunderstandings/Misuses
May neglect practical application in favor of emphasis on accuracy of analysis
Imparting research details may bore others
Can rely too much on reasoning/too little on spiritual insight
Tends to discount insights and practical wisdom of uneducated people
May become too fact-oriented rather than people-oriented
As critical thinkers, may appear sarcastic or negative

The Gift of Propecy

Focus: Right and Wrong; Obedience to God's Word
Primary Misuse: Legalism and/or Condemnation

Positive/Identifying Characteristics
Willing, even when afraid, to take strong and sometimes unpopular stands
Sees need of group as a whole over against need of individuals
Deep concern for reputation/programs of God
Heart-broken over sins of people and society
Cultivates the art of hearing God speak
Persistent and impatient in expressing concern and bringing about solutions

Misunderstandings/Misuses
May obscure message of Who they represent in zeal to defend a cause
Some feel they have divine right to be pushy
Right/wrong focus may become judgmental
Quick conclusions may foster incorrect opinions
Strict standards may hinder intimate relationships
Self-critical; may feel left out and become overly defensive

*This handout draws upon material from Dr. Robert Clinton, *Spiritual Gifts* (Canada: Horizon House, 1985).

The Gift of Exhortation

Focus: Growth toward Potential
Primary Misuse: Relying on Experience or Method

Positive/Identifying Characteristics

Outlines logical, precise steps of action
Sees individual needs in group situation
Discerns people's Spiritual level and meets them there
Deep dissatisfaction with superficial truth or information systems without practical application
Interprets Scripture in light of experience
Sensitive ability to relate how people's problems can produce great maturity

Misunderstandings/Misuses

Desire for lifestyle witness may appear to be lack of interest in evangelism
Focus on practical application may take Scripture out of context
Emphasizing action may disregard feelings
Danger of creating dependence on exhorter rather than on God
Tends to categorize problems and thus may reach premature conclusions
May dominate conversation by giving advice and a plan for every problem

The Gift of Helps

Focus: Practical Service
Primary Misuse: Over-Extension and Exhaustion

Positive/Identifying Characteristics

Meets needs as quickly as possible
Joy in serving "behind-the-scenes"
Takes action (not merely plans) to meet needs
Enjoys short-range and finishing projects; frustrated with long-term or incomplete
Often feels inadequate/unqualified for spiritual leadership
Enjoys manual projects; needs clear instructions

Misunderstandings/Misuses

May interfere with other's need to help self
Avoiding "red tape" may circumvent proper authority to get job done
Eagerness to serve may prompt suspicion of self-advancement
Tends to criticize those who do not recognize/meet obvious needs
Finds difficulty in delegating
Can be moody or stubborn if not appreciated

The Gift of Giving

Focus: Stewardship; Providing Financial and Material Resources
Primary Misuse: Controlling and Manipulating People and Ministries

Positive/Identifying Characteristics

Makes wise investments for more to give
Gives quietly, without recognition/publicity
Joy when gift is answer to specific prayer
Concern for high-quality gifts
Tends to be personally frugal, content
Sense of fulfillment in support of others' ministries

Misunderstandings/Misuses

Concern for money may appear materialistic
Ability to give may lead to spiritual pride
Pressuring others who do not have their ability to give
Danger of deception by those who would take advantage of their gift
May prevent others' growth if too generous
Donating to "projects" rather than involvement/concern with people's needs

The Gift of Administation

Focus: Organizing and Managing Systems
Primary Misuse: Relying on Programs; "Systems" More Important than People

Positive/Identifying Characteristics

Good at designing smooth-running systems
Enjoys organizing things (sometimes, people)
Knows what can/cannot be delegated
Takes control if no structured leadership exists
Endures adverse reaction to accomplish goals
Occasionally (but not often) accompanied by gift of leadership

Misunderstandings/Misuses

May see people as objects to reach goal
Frustration with inefficiency may promote taking charge prematurely
Insensitive to needs/schedules of others
May ignore character faults in good workers
By enduring criticism may become closed to valid suggestion/complaints
Function of leading without leadership gift can have disastrous consequences

The Gift of Pastor/Shepherd

Focus: Protecting the Flock
Primary Misuse: Over-Extension, Burn-Out, Difficulty Delegating

Positive/Identifying Characteristics

Recognizes a sense of calling to care for a particular group of people
Influences by actions and proper behavior
Looks at a group, sees its problems, and knows how to bring solutions
Guides fellow believers by sharing Scriptures and praying with/for them
Makes effort to reach the lost and restore backslidden believers
Derives strength from prayer, praise, and study of God's Word

Misunderstandings/Misuses

May push or demand rather than lead
When discouraged, may view those being served as the "enemy"
Responsibilities of leadership may cause withdrawal and isolation
Ability to inspire loyalty runs danger of taking advantage of others for personal gain
Pride may grow and interfere with recognition and resolution of personal weaknesses
Others may worship pastor rather than God

HINT:

The "Gift Lists" in Scripture.

Romans 12:6-8
1 Corinthians 12:7-11
1 Corinthians 12:28
Ephesians 4:11-12

DRIVING WHAT...TO WHERE?

You have been awarded a grand prize: a new vehicle of your choice, plus vouchers for gasoline, meals, and lodging at your chosen destination—and a month off with pay from your employer.

1. What kind of vehicle would you choose? What options?
2. Where would you go? Why?

Sharing Your Prize: If you won such a prize, would you take the trip? If you also had the choice of taking several people with you, who would you take—and why?

KEY CONCEPTS
on High-Voltage Power

#1 We receive _____ from the Holy Spirit for the purpose of _____ _____ _____.

#2 The Body of Christ is complete only when all its parts are_____ _____.

#3 We each must _____ our parts and how they work with the_____ _____ _____.

THINK IT OVER

Our gifts might be compared to vehicles that God provides to take us to a "destination"—the service He designed us to do. We might relate our Driving Force Gift(s) to a type of vehicle, such as an all-terrain vehicle, a mini-van, a pick-up, a sports car, or a sedan. It will determine the primary function God has designed us to do in ministry. The other gifts in our cluster might be compared to the vehicle's options—a sun roof or convertible top, automatic or 5-speed transmission, color, trim, upholstery, how many cylinders, etc. *Options add distinction to a vehicle but do not alter its basic function.*

Whatever "vehicle" you have been given, three things are common to all: (1) they have great worth, (2) they have been freely given, and (3) they are meant to be shared.

But you will receive power when the Holy Spirit comes on you; and you will be my witnesses in Jerusalem, and in all Judea and Samaria, and to the ends of the earth.
—Acts 1:8

As a prisoner for the Lord, then, I urge you to live a life worthy of the calling you have received.
—Ephesians 4:1

Now the body is not made up of one part but of many. 15 If the foot should say, "Because I am not a hand, I do not belong to the body," it would not for that reason cease to be part of the body. 16 And if the ear should say, "Because I am not an eye, I do not belong to the body," it would not for that reason cease to be part of the body. 17 If the whole body were an eye, where would the sense of hearing be? If the whole body were an ear, where would the sense of smell be? 18 But in fact God has arranged the parts in the body, every one of them, just as he wanted them to be. 19 If they were all one part, where would the body be? 20 As it is, there are many parts, but one body. 21 The eye cannot say to the hand, "I don't need you!" And the head cannot say to the feet, "I don't need you!" 22 On the contrary, those parts of the body that seem to be weaker are indispensable, 23 and the parts that we think are less honorable we treat with special honor. And the parts that are unpresentable are treated with special modesty, 24 while our presentable parts need no special treatment. But God has combined the members of the body and has given greater honor to the parts that lacked it, 25 so that there should be no division in the body, but that its parts should have equal concern for each other.
—1 Corinthians 12:14-25

47

But you will receive power when the Holy Spirit comes on you; and you will be my witnesses in Jerusalem, and in all Judea and Samaria, and to the ends of the earth.
—Acts 1:8

As a prisoner for the Lord, then, I urge you to live a life worthy of the calling you have received.
—Ephesians 4:1

Now the body is not made up of one part but of many. 15 If the foot should say, "Because I am not a hand, I do not belong to the body," it would not for that reason cease to be part of the body. 16 And if the ear should say, "Because I am not an eye, I do not belong to the body," it would not for that reason cease to be part of the body. 17 If the whole body were an eye, where would the sense of hearing be? If the whole body were an ear, where would the sense of smell be? 18 But in fact God has arranged the parts in the body, every one of them, just as he wanted them to be. 19 If they were all one part, where would the body be? 20 As it is, there are many parts, but one body. 21 The eye cannot say to the hand, "I don't need you!" And the head cannot say to the feet, "I don't need you!" 22 On the contrary, those parts of the body that seem to be weaker are indispensable, 23 and the parts that we think are less honorable we treat with special honor. And the parts that are unpresentable are treated with special modesty, 24 while our presentable parts need no special treatment. But God has combined the members of the body and has given greater honor to the parts that lacked it, 25 so that there should be no division in the body, but that its parts should have equal concern for each other.
—1 Corinthians 12:14-25

48

THIS DESCRIBES ME BEST...
Which of the following phrases best describes you? (Select the top one or two.)

___ I share my faith with unbelievers
___ I comfort people who are hurting
___ I love studying the Scriptures
___ I tend to follow the rules
___ I see potential in everyone
___ I enjoy hands-on tasks
___ I save money so I can give more
___ I organize everything
___ I watch out for others' welfare

•*Share your selection in groups of 3 or 4. Give a recent example or experience in your life that confirms your choice.*

WHAT DRIVES YOU?
Look at the lines you checked above that describe you best. Each description relates to the focus of a Driving Force Gift. On the handout "The Driving Force Gifts," find the focus that relates to the line you have checked. Read the characteristics and potential misunderstandings of that gift.

•*Does this gift fit you?*
•*Compare notes with two or three people. Do the descriptions fit each of you? Why, or why not?*

KEY CONCEPTS
on High-Voltage Power

#1 We receive _____ from the Holy Spirit for the purpose of _____ _____ _____.

#2 The Body of Christ is complete only when all its parts are_____ _____.

#3 We each must _____ our parts and how they work with the_____ ___ _____.

IN OTHER WORDS...

Spiritual gifts are God's way of administering His grace to others. When we exercise our gifts, we function as the hands and feet of Christ.
—Charles Stanley

People are motivated to action for two reasons: either they have to or they want to. Spiritual gifts are the "want to" of Christian service.
— Larry Gilbert, *How to Find Meaning and Fulfillment through Understanding the Spiritual Gift Within You*

(CONTINUES FLIPSIDE)

Take Home Page

BRINGING THE LESSON HOME

How can you indentify, verify, and develop your gifts? Ask yourself questions like these:

___ What work do you seem drawn to do?
___ What unmet needs grieve your heart most?
___ Do opportunities occur to use this gift?
___ Do you see positive results when you use the gift?
___ Are you willing to answer the Spirit's call?
___ How well do others receive the work of the gift?
___ Who uses the gift well and can mentor you?

•*Ponder each Driving Force Gift. Where might it be used in your church or community?*

GETTING INTO ACTION

This week I will take the following deliberate action(s):

___ Journal my insights about Driving Force Gifts
___ Ask _____ to help verify my gifts
___ Look around to see where I might serve best
___ Get a book and do more reading about gifts
___ Attempt to identify gifts of others around me
___ Seek a mentor who maturely uses my gift(s)
___ Consider how my gifts apply at work
___ Brainstorm with my roommate to identify our gifts
___ Observe the potential gifts of my children
___ Other: _____

SHAPE UP!

Over the course of this study, we'er looking at how God forms each of us with unique combinations of attributes, which form our "SHAPE" for service. Can you fill in the blanks?

S _____ **Gifts**
The "what" we do in ministry. (Session 2)

H _____ **'s Desires**
The "where" we do our ministry. (Session 4)

A _____
Our physical, mental, emotional resouces. (Session 4)

P _____ **Style**
Our unique way of being and relating. (Session 5)

E _____
How God instructs, guides, and matures us. (Session 6)

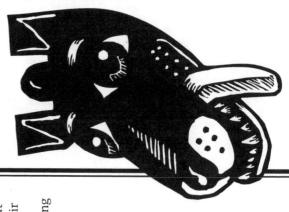

IN OTHER WORDS...

The Lord's Army is not a volunteer army. The question is not, "Will you volunteer for the Lord's Army?" The question is, "Are you a draft dodger or not?" If you are a Christian, you are in His Army whether you want to be or not. —Larry Gilbert

Take Home Page MARCH continued

DAILY READINGS AND REFLECTIONS

This week, take a few minutes to ponder each day's thought regarding spiritual gifts.

Monday—Spiritual gifts are different than fruit of the Spirit. Gifts relate to ministry; fruit relates to maturity. We can use our gifts immaturely. Read the fruit of the spirit in Galatians 5:22-23. As we mature in our faith, God produces increasing measures of fruit of the Spirit. How's your fruit?

Tuesday—Do you desire to know God's will for your life? Read Romans 12:1-6. Paul says that as we devote our bodies and minds to our loving God, He will enable us to know His will. Then Paul proceeds to teach about knowing and using our gifts. Being in God's will involves using our spiritual gifts!

Wednesday—Review the truth that God expects us to use what we have been given. Read 1 Corinthians 4:1-4. Is it your heart's motive to faithfully use what has been entrusted to you?

Thursday—Do you realize that you have a calling from God? Read Ephesians 4:1-12. Paul urges us to action—to living a life worthy of our calling. In response to the grace we have received from God, we are called to use the gifts He has given us.

Friday—Did you know that serving will bring you joy? Read John 15:9-13. Obeying Jesus' commands does not just mean doing the "thou shalt's" and not doing the "thou shalt not's." It means laying down our lives in serving each other.

Saturday—Do you want to become more like Jesus? In Luke 12:35-37, Jesus cautions us to live our lives in such a manner that we are ready for service. He will reward us for our faithfulness.

'DRIVING FORCE GIFT' MINI-EVALUATION

Imagine that you are joining a church or ministry staff in full-time Christian service. All the ministries below will be provided by the organization, but you are to devote your time and spend your energy in one primary area. Which would you choose? (If you can't choose just one, select two, but no more than three.)

1. Exposing or helping to expose sin, proclaiming righteousness and warning of judgment.

2. Demonstrating Christ's love by meeting practical needs of church members and nonbelievers.

3. Accurately researching and systematically explaining the doctrines of the Bible.

4. Presenting practical, "how-to" studies to help people apply Scriptural principles to daily living.

5. Providing funds and material resources for individual, church and/or parachurch ministries.

6. Designing systems to enable every ministry to be done effectively and in order.

7. Understanding and nurturing those who are suffering, whether believers or nonbelievers.

8. Encouraging believers to actively seek out the lost and equipping them to share their faith.

9. Overseeing, "coaching," training and caring for a group of believers on an ongoing basis.

Read the words below—backwards—to find what your Driving Force Gift may be.

1. Ycehporp
2. Ecivres
3. Gnihcaet
4. Noitatrohxe
5. Gnivig
6. Noitartsinimda
7. Ycrem
8. Msilegnave
9. Gnirotsap

Session 4
Wouldja? Couldja?
YEAH! DO IT!

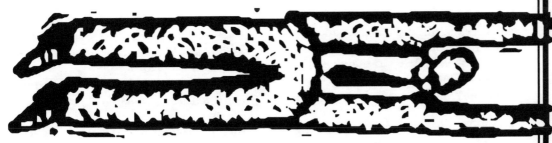

SESSION AIM

To help singles seek meaningful areas of service through using their natural abilities to respond to their heart's motives and concerns.

Have you heard about the animal school? The ACLU (Animal Competence Leveling University) taught a multi-discipline, standardized curriculum of running, swimming, flying, and climbing. An owl who valued wisdom was the instructor. A duck, eagle, squirrel, and rabbit enrolled.

The duck loved swimming and flying, but he waddled when he ran and couldn't climb at all. Yet the serious little duck practiced climbing until the webs on one foot were torn and he swam around in circles. The eagle flew majestically, but his running was marginal and he almost drowned in his first swim. The squirrel was a passionate climber and runner, but the other students almost laughed him out of school when he got wet. And the rabbit? His only zeal was running. A compulsive over-achiever, he worked hard at the other subjects, but failed. He became too depressed to run.

The school was closed at the end of the year because all failed their final exams.

The moral is obvious. Like the animals in the story, people have passions and abilities that lead them to serve in particular areas. While an area of service is exhilarating and effective for one, it may be exhausting and futile for another.

As we seek to discover where God has designed us to serve, two important ingredients to consider are our heart-desires and our natural abilities.

WHAT'S IT ALL ABOUT?

As you move through your session, keep in mind these Key Concepts you'll be conveying to your group members:

• God provides internal guidance toward the work He would have us do.
• God both motivates and fulfills the desires of our hearts.
• Our abilities are gifts from God.
• God builds teams of people with complementary abilities.

BIBLE REFERENCES:

Philippians 2:13
Psalm 37:4
Exodus 31:2-6

51

1—Let's Get Started
(5-10 minutes)

Option 1: Awareness of Ourselves?
Needed: Interactive Page #1.

1. Distribute Interactive Page #1 and have everyone fill in the blanks under "Causes And Competencies." After a few minutes, ask volunteers to share whether it was easy or difficult to make their lists—and tell why. Then discuss in small groups:

•*In your opinion, are most people aware of their natural abilities—or do people tend to take themselves for granted?*
•*Why is your most important cause so significant to you?*

Option 2: Dream Time
Needed: Interactive Page #1.

1. Refer to the exercise titled "Medal of Accomplishment." Allow time for everyone to develop their dream and note what they did, and how they did it. Then ask people to share their stories with a small group.

2. Point out that some people are keenly aware of the causes that they value and of their abilities, while others have difficulty listing causes or abilities—or both. Part of determining where God would have us serve is knowing the heart-causes and abilities He has given us.

2—Looking to the Word
(15 minutes)

Draw from "What the Bible Has to Say," on pages 56-58. Use the introduction to examine why it is important to be aware of our heart and abilities. As you move into the transition and teaching the Key Concepts, refer participants to the blanks on their Interactive Pages.

3—Applying It to My Life
(5-10 minutes)

1. Reform small groups from Step 1. Refer to "In Other Words" on Interactive Page #1. Ask everyone to read Marge Caldwell's statement, then reflect on these questions:

•*Look at the causes and/or dreams you have listed. How are you using, or how could you use, your abilities to help bring about those causes or dreams?*

2. Now ask everyone to choose a cause of greatest concern to them and discuss:

•*What would it mean to you to be involved in this cause?*
•*How would your heart-desire be fulfilled if you could make a difference there?*
•*Which of your abilities might be used to serve that cause?*

4—Taking the Next Step
(5 minutes)

Needed: Flip chart or chalkboard.

1. Record the causes that are important to your group members. Look for one or two that are common to several in the group. Form a Task Force to meet during the coming week in order to explore service objectives. The group members should talk about how they could combine their abilities to meet their objective.

2. Next week they should report back their findings and enlist others' involvement. If possible, implement a plan of action that can begin before Session Six. Those who participated may then relate their ministry experiences.

5—Let's Wrap It Up
(5 minutes)

Needed: Take Home Page.

1. Distribute the Take Home Page and draw attention to the exercises regarding Heart and Abilities.

2. Ask group members to reform their discussion groups and to pass their Interactive Pages to persons on their right. If your group members are comfortable praying with each other, ask them to take turns praying for the person whose sheet they have received—that each will find a way to use his or her abilities in the areas of their heart-causes.

HINT:

When preparing to teach "Looking to the Word," rehearse in advance. Watch your time closely. Present any appropriate material from "Going Deeper" that will fit in your time frame. Use the conclusion to spur participants to begin to take action on the Key Concepts.

When You Have More Time...
(How to Use This Material in 60-90 Minutes)
Example: Small Groups at Home

1—Let's Get Started
(5-10 minutes)

Option 1: Team-working Channels
Needed: A strip of construction paper for each person, one marble for each group, and one paper cup for each group.

Form a long line and give each person a 1" x 12" strip of construction paper. Fold the strip in half, lengthwise. Explain to the group members that they will be given a marble and must create a channel for the marble to travel from the starting point into a paper cup at the finish point. Specify that the channels can only move up or down, not sideways, and they must make contact with one another when the marble is transferred. Work together to make it work! Let everyone know that "a good team"—one that can really concentrate—should be able to do it in about five tries. Then discuss:

•*What things do you concentrate on most—to make your life flow smoothly along? To what extent do you follow your heart's desires?*

Option 2: Discussion
Use the questions on Interactive Page #2, under "Interact #1." Have small groups discuss their responses and then report to the large group.

2—Looking to the Word
(20-25 minutes)

Present the material found in "Presenting What the Bible Has to Say," on pages 56-58. Divide your allotted time into three segments: (1) Introduction, (2) Key Concepts, and (3) Conclusion. Keep your presentation short and simple. Hit the highlights, drawing upon the "Going Deeper" information as appropriate

3—Applying It to My Life
(20-25 minutes)

Needed: Interactive page #2.

1. Once you complete your presentation, form small groups of three to four people and direct attention to "The Value of Teamwork" on Interactive Page #2. Ask participants to make notes and then discuss their responses.

2. Now get people involved in "Sure, I Enjoyed That!" Allow time for all to reflect and note their responses. Ask everyone to brainstorm together about how their abilities could be used to impact their causes.

4—Taking the Next Step
(10-20 minutes)

Needed: Take Home Page.

1. Distribute the Take Home Page and conduct an exercise in silence. Ask everyone to take a few moments to respond to "Looking Outward" and to "My God-Given Abilities," then to remain silent and wait for further instructions.

2. When people have completed the exercises, ask them to pray silently for God's help in recognizing the causes that are important to them—and for courage to take action and get involved.

3. Follow the time of silence with this exercise: Distribute index cards. Have everyone write for themselves an assignment that they can do this coming week, to begin or move toward, getting involved. Ask them to bring the card back next week and to report on whether they have followed through with their plan.

5—Let's Wrap It Up
(5 minutes)

1. Make your group's announcements and then call attention to "The Diagnosis? I Dunno!" exercise for any who may be struggling to identify their causes and abilities. Encourage them to complete "Looking Inward: My Heart-Motivations" (on the Take Home Page) during the coming week.

2. Close in prayer.

HINT:

If your group is newly-formed, people should be getting comfortable with each other by this week.
Encourage transparency and mutual acceptance by modeling those actions.

Extending The Learning...

(How to Use This Material in Two Hours)

Example: Extended Week-Night Program

HINT:

Begin to urge your group to action. Entrust faithful members with ministry tasks and watch them grow.

1—Let's Get Started

(20-30 minutes)

Option 1: Causes and Competencies
Needed: Interactive Page #1.

Form small groups and distribute Interactive Page #1. When everyone has filled in the spaces under "Causes and Competencies," form groups to discuss peoples' earliest recollections of concern for their causes. After a few minutes, ask:

> •*Have the abilities you've listed seemed "to come naturally"?*
> > •*Or have you worked to develop a skill that was difficult at first?*

Option 2: Could I Do That?
Needed: Interactive Page #2.

In small groups, allow time for everyone to recall and note the two sets of circumstances and emotions in "Could I Do That?" on Interactive Page #2. Ask participants to share *what they hated most* about the first experience and *what they loved most* about the second.

Option 3: Placard Fun

Use the activity titled "Construct-A-Placard" in the Extra Options, page 59.

2—Looking to the Word

(20 minutes)

Present the material in "Looking to the Word." Design your Introduction to hook the group's interest. Add information as appropriate from Going Deeper. Watch your time carefully to draw to a conclusion on schedule.

3—Applying It to My Life

(30-40 minutes)

1. When you're through presenting "Looking to the Word," have everyone refer to the Take Home Page and take a few minutes to read and do "Looking Inward: My Heart-Motivations." Allow time for everyone to complete the exercise. Then ask them to disclose to each other their top-

ranking motivations and to explore what part of teamwork those motivations might lead them to do.

2. If you used the opener "Construct-A-Placard," reform those same small groups. Point to these sections on the Take Home Page: "Looking Outward: My Heart-Causes," "Looking Inward: My Heart-Motivations" and "My God-Given Abilities."

Ask each person to consider the name his or her group chose and the task on their card. Ask them to ponder, then discuss what heart-cause might have brought that team together and what heart-motivations and abilities might apply to their part on the team. (This exercise can be especially funny if they have chosen something silly like "Daisy-Pickers Anonymous" for their group name.)

4—Taking the Next Step

(30-40 minutes)

Needed: Take Home Page.

Refer to "Looking Outward: My Heart-Causes" on the Take Home Page. Ask everyone to consider all three questions, but to make notes only on the one that is easiest to answer. Have people share their response with the group. Ask them also to consider how they might make a difference in that cause.

5—Let's Wrap It Up

(5-10 minutes)

1. Make your group's announcements at this time.

2. Close by reading Psalm 139:1-18, 23-24 aloud. Thank God for His wonderful creation in each person in your group. Ask Him to search each heart and reveal His plan to each of you. If your group is comfortable with it, call for "hugs all around."

My Personal Game Plan

STEP 1 | Time: _____ minutes.

Materials Needed:

Activities Summary:

STEP 2 | Time: _____ minutes.

Materials Needed:

Activities Summary:

STEP 3 | Time: _____ minutes.

Materials Needed:

Activities Summary:

STEP 4 | Time: _____ minutes.

Materials Needed:

Activities Summary:

STEP 5 | Time: _____ minutes.

Materials Needed:

Activities Summary:

Just for You
Teacher's Devotional

George (not his real name) was a strange man, socially inept. His first few weeks in class, he stood against the wall, as if it would collapse were it not for his presence. A few noticed him; most were busy with their friends and ignored him.

The group leader got to know George—his story of childhood abuse, his dependence on alcohol. The leader chose to love George. She encouraged him, including him in her own personal circle of friendships. She modeled unconditional love. She discovered George's abilities and found a place for him to serve.

Within a few months, God changed George. He accepted Jesus as his personal Savior. He stopped drinking. He led his kids to the Lord. He formed friendships.

Several months later, on a Single Adult Emphasis Sunday, George shared his testimony with the congregation. As a newcomer, George had felt like "a bug in a jar." But one leader became "Jesus with skin on." George was never again the same—and neither were those who knew him.

Love your group unconditionally. Pray for them. Dream dreams for them. "And if anyone gives even a cup of cold water to one of these little ones because he is my disciple, I tell you the truth, he will certainly not lose his reward" (Matt. 10:42).

—*Lana Wilkinson*

MY GOALS FOR THIS SESSION:

- TO HELP SINGLE ADULTS
  _____
  _____
  _____

- TO HELP SINGLE ADULTS
  _____
  _____
  _____

- TO HELP SINGLE ADULTS
  _____
  _____
  _____

- TO HELP SINGLE ADULTS
  _____
  _____
  _____

WHAT I LEARNED FROM READING 'LOOKING TO THE WORD' . . .

Notes and Insights—

Presenting
What the Bible Has to Say...

Here's your mini-lecture covering the biblical Key Concepts. Try to become familiar with the flow of thoughts, and the outline, in order to present this material with maximum eye contact. Special instructions to you are in bold type. (Note: Have group members refer to the Key Concepts section on their Interactive Page. They may wish to fill in the blanks as you speak.)

Introduction

Each person has a unique physical heartbeat. Physicians monitor health changes by comparing current and past electrocardiograms—but even when health changes, the heart's basic pattern remains the same.

We also have a unique emotional and spiritual "heartbeat." It races when we encounter activities, circumstances, or subjects that interest us. This God-given internal guidance system draws us to specific interests and has much to do with revealing how God has designed us to serve.

We exercise to increase our physical heart rate and benefit our physical health. Involvement in interests that stimulate our emotional heartbeat benefits our emotional and spiritual health.

*Henry J. M. Nouwen, *Can You Drink the Cup?* (Notre Dame: Ave Maria Press, 1996).

Ask someone to read Philippians 2:13.

THE KEY CONCEPTS

Transition statement: Each of us has God-given heart-desires and abilities. Heart-desires inspire our interior motivations and draw us to exterior causes. Abilities are the physical, mental, emotional, and relational tools with which we function. *The work God has designed us to do will fulfill our heart-desires and utilize our natural abilities.*

When God motivates our hearts to become involved in meeting a particular need, He also gives us the ability to do our part in meeting that need. Today's lesson examines the next two elements of how God "SHAPE'd" us for service: Heart-desires and Abilities.

On the chalkboard, place this diagram:

Spiritual Gifts	**God designed**
H_____	**my**
A_____	**"SHAPE"**
Personal Styles	**for**
Experiences	**Service!**

As we seek to discover where God has designed us to serve, two important ingredients to consider are our heart-desires and our abilities. Let's look at four key concepts related to these ingredients...

KEY CONCEPT #1:
God provides internal guidance toward the work He would have us do.

Have you noticed that some people are passionate about concerns that are of little interest to you—and vice versa? God creates us with different passions, so that we each may help meet needs that are uniquely important to our hearts.

Illustration. Henri Nouwen, a priest, had taught at such prestigious universities as Notre Dame, Yale, and Harvard. In his mid-50s he left the world of academia to serve as pastor of L'Arche Daybreak, a residence facility in Toronto for people with severe mental disabilities.

Nouwen describes meeting Adam, a 22-year-old man who could not speak, walk alone, or show signs of recognition, and who suffered from daily epileptic seizures. When he first met Adam, Nouwen was afraid and wanted to avoid him. After a few months of caring for Adam—waking him in the morning, bathing him, brushing his teeth, shaving his beard and feeding him breakfast—Nouwen's heart changed. "Knowing Adam became a privilege for me," Nouwen writes. "Who can spend a few hours each day with a man who gives you all his confidence and trust? Isn't that what joy is?"*

You may never serve with the seriously handicapped, but you may be certain that when God guides you to do His work, He also will give you joy in doing it!

Ask someone to read Psalm 37:4. Then state:

KEY CONCEPT #2:
God both motivates and fulfills the desires of our hearts.

This passage is much like the question, "Which came first, the chicken or the egg?" As we delight in the Lord, we recognize and respond to heart-desires that He has placed in us. As we respond to the heart-desires He places in us, our deepest needs are fulfilled. As our desires are fulfilled, our delight in the Lord is increased, and the cycle repeats.

•Think: What are the desires of your heart right now? To what extent are they being fulfilled in the work and service you perform?

Read Exodus 31:2-6. Then say: There are two important thoughts in this passage:

KEY CONCEPT #3:
Our abilities are gifts from God.

God had been giving detailed instructions to Moses about building the tabernacle and its furnishings. To accomplish His work, God called those who had the abilities necessary to do the job.

If you have time, take a moment to clarify the distinction between spiritual gifts and natural abilities, something about which students may be confused:

While interpretations differ on which functions are spiritual gifts and which are abilities, it is important to understand that gifts and abilities are two very different capacities. Heart-desires and abilities are found in all people. All can respond to motives and causes God has planted in their hearts. All can use their abilities to help society and their neighbors and families.

Remember that spiritual gifts are manifestations of the Holy Spirit working through believers' lives to enable the Church to execute its task on earth. Secular organizations can accomplish good for society. The unique task of the Church, however, is to reach people, mature Christians, and organize people to reach and mature others. Both abilities and spiritual gifts are required to do the work of the Church.

KEY CONCEPT #4:
God builds teams of people with complementary abilities.

Notice that while Moses was given the vision and supervised the work, "Bez" was given the hands-on abilities needed for the job. "Ollie" and the other craftsmen also had skills they could use. God brought together a team with skills necessary for the work He called them to do. Each person's skills complemented and enhanced the others'.

We don't hear much about Bez and Ollie, but without their skills, Moses and the priests could not have done what God called them to do. Just as Moses and the priests could not accomplish God's work alone, neither can today's church leaders. A big job requires a team effort.

HINT:

Those who receive information visually tend to retain what they see. Filling in the blanks assists those who learn through action. A final summary by having participants voice the words in the blanks reinforces those who learn by hearing.

Conclusion

God still calls and equips us to be small parts of big works! As you seek to discover your part, spend some time contemplating: (1) your heart causes and motives—your internal guidance to "where-and-why" to serve; and (2) your abilities—physical, mental, emotional and relational tools that determine "how" you serve. Many Christians struggle to find God's will, not realizing that His will is reflected in His design of our lives.

Wouldja? Detect your internal motivations. Be aware of the causes and desires that tug at your heart. *Couldja?* Celebrate the abilities God has given you. Use them for His glory! Wouldja? Couldja? Yeah! Do It!

GOING DEEPER

Note on Philippians 2:13. *Energeo,* the Greek word translated "works" in Philippians 1:13, means to be active, to be fervently effectual, to be powerful. The word translated "will" (*thelo*) means to determine as an active option from subjective impulse; to choose, to desire.* Thus, God actively, fervently shows Himself in us to cause us to actively choose and desire, then to act upon His good purpose. In other words, God is serious about directing us to carry out His work! Our challenge is to align our active will with His. He will not *force* us to do what we are called to do.

Note on Psalm 37:4. One way of submitting to God's will is to delight in Him. A word study of the Hebrew for "delight," "give," "desires," and "heart," shows we are to be soft and pliable, luxuriating in God's presence. Then, He will both cause and grant requests that flow from the very center of our being. We choose whether to follow God's plan and allow Him to mold us. We choose whether to spend time in His presence. When we submit to Him, our desires are both aligned with His desires and fulfilled by Him.

Note on Exodus 31:3-6. Disagreements exist as to whether certain functions are spiritual gifts or abilities. This is a passage with varied interpretations. Some consider craftsmanship a spiritual gift, interpreting "filled him with the Spirit of God" as mean-

ing: "bestowed him with a spiritual gift" (identified as craftsmanship).

However, the Hebrew *ruwach* translated "spirit" in this passage, means breath, exhalation, spirit of a rational being (including its expression and functions). The balance of the words refer to wisdom, intelligence, cunning, and an ability to do work as an occupation.* Thus it appears that a more accurate interpretation is that God breathed life into Bezalel and also gave him abilities, not a spiritual gift.

Note on Pride vs. Humility. Some Christians confuse awareness of their abilities with pride. Misunderstanding humility, they down play their God-given skills and talents. C. S. Lewis eloquently addresses this issue in his classic *Screwtape Letters.* In this allegory, Screwtape (Satan) proposes to Wormwood (his devils) effective strategies to defeat God (the Enemy) and Christians (the patient).

"You must . . . conceal from the patient the true end of Humility. Let him think of it not as self-forgetfulness, but as a certain kind of opinion (namely, a low opinion) of his own talents and character. Some talents, I gather, he really has. Fix in his mind the idea that humility consists in trying to believe those talents to be less valuable than he believes them to be...

"To anticipate the Enemy's strategy, we must consider His aims. The Enemy wants to bring the man to a state of mind in which he could design the best cathedral in the world, and know it to be the best, and rejoice in the fact, without being any more (or less) or otherwise glad at having done it than He would be if it had been done by another. The Enemy wants him, in the end, to be so free from any bias in his own favour that he can rejoice in his own talents as frankly and gratefully as in his neighbor's talents—or in a sunrise, an elephant, or a waterfall." +

*WORDsearch Bible Study Software, version 3.18. Copyright 1987-1995, NavPress Software.

+C. S. Lewis, Screwtape Letters

EXTRA OPTIONS

Pick and Choose any of the following to fit the needs of your group...

Options to Consider...for Step 1

Construct-A-Placard

Advance preparation: For each group of six people, provide one letter-size blank card, one felt marker. For all to share, provide one 2-hole punch, one scissors, and one ball of yarn. Prepare sets of 6 cards with the following instructions—

#1 You are resourceful and have a blank sign
 #2 You can write
 #3 You can promote cooperation
 #4 You can do crafts
 #5 You can perform
 #6 You can coordinate

Prepare the following instruction sheet for each group:

Lead your group to select a group name. Then, give the following instructions:
 #1—donate your sign. #2—write the group name on the sign. #3—borrow the hole punch and scissors. #4—punch 2 holes in the sign; cut enough yarn to tie one end to each hole in the paper. #5—model the sign.

Hand out the cards randomly and have participants form teams of people with cards numbered 1 through 6. (To save time, form groups of 6 and then hand each group a set of cards.) Tell everyone that they may do only the job that is described on their card. Give #1 the blank letter-size card, #2 the marker, and #6 the instruction sheet.
 Chances are 5 out of 6 that you will have one incomplete group. If so, they will discover their inability to complete the task. When placards are complete, divulge that one group was unable to complete its assignment. Pose the question, "In a 'real life' scenario, how might this group have gotten the job done?"
 Make this point: God places certain causes on our hearts. He gives us the abilities to do what He calls us to do. When our skills are inadequate, He enables us or brings someone else to serve in partnership with us.

Options to Consider...for Step 3

Subduing Screwtape—Form groups of three to four people. If you read the excerpt from *Screwtape Letters*, bring home the point that Satan wages a battle in our minds to defeat our work before we even get started.
 Ask everyone to silently reflect for a moment and note on their Interactive Page what mental struggles they have with getting involved in ministry. What are their fears, their hesitations, their hang-ups? After they have made notes for themselves, ask them to share their mental battle with their group and to pray for each other to have courage to "subdue Screwtape."

Debate: What Makes Me Tick?
Needed: 15 slips of paper, each listing one of the 15 Heart-Motivations; a container for a drawing; two note pads and pens per group.

HINT:

Manage your groups' discussions by "wandering around." Listen to the hearts of your single adults. Seek to understand what is important in their circumstances. Cast the vision that they can make a difference!

Form small groups and distribute the Take Home Page before having each group draw two or three slips. Ask all to study the descriptions of their group's words in "Looking Inward: My Heart-Motivations." Then have half of each group brainstorm and note how their group's motivations can be used for good; the other half, for bad. When the lists are made, take turns having the groups debate whether using that motivation is "good" or "bad." The point? Each God-given motivation can be used for good or for evil.

Option to Consider...for Step 4

A Work of Art

Advance preparation: Bring either blank paper and a selection of markers or crayons and/or Play-Doh®. Also bring an index card for each person. Form groups of 3-4 and give the following instructions:

Draw a picture or make a sculpture representing one of your important heart-causes. Do another picture or sculpture representing your abilities that could be used to serve that cause.

When everyone has finished, first guess what each other's artwork represents, then disclose the meaning of your work.

After everyone has had time to share, distribute the index cards. Ask the group members to brainstorm with each other about how they might move from idea to action. Ask each person to write the best ideas from the brainstorming session about how they could use their abilities to impact their causes. Ask them to commit to prayerfully consider their own options and to pray for the other members in their group during the coming week.

Options to Consider...for Step 5

"Do It" Wave—Form a large circle. Divide it into four equal segments; number the segments 1 through 4. Assign the following words as numbered, one to each section:

1. Wouldja?
2. Couldja?
3. Yeah!
4. Do it!

Stand in the middle and lead the group to do a "Wouldja?-Couldja?-Yeah!-Do It!" progressive wave. Repeat several times, encouraging them to crank up the volume and animation with each wave. Get into the rhythm; stomp your feet; clap your hands. Get radical!

Close with a prayer, asking the Lord to help your group get excited about being part of His team.

Connection with Yarn

Needed: a large ball of yarn.

Form a large circle. Roll out several feet of yarn, hold the loose end, and pass the ball across the circle to someone, saying something positive about his or her abilities. That person will then roll out several feet of yarn, hold onto the string and pass the ball with a positive comment to another individual. Repeat the process, with each person continuing to hold onto the string, until everyone in the circle is connected. Explain that we all are connected in the Body of Christ. When each person shares his or her heart and abilities with the group, the ministry becomes stronger.

CAUSES AND COMPETENCIES

List three causes that are important to you:

1.
2.
3.

List three of your strongest abilities (physical, mental, emotional, or relational):

1.
2.
3.

KEY CONCEPTS
on Heart-Desires and Abilities

#1 God provides _____ _____ toward the work He would have us do.

#2 God both _____ and _____ the desires of our hearts.

#3 Our _____ are gifts from God.

#4 God builds teams of people with _____ _____.

MEDAL OF ACCOMPLISHMENT

Dream for a moment. Your local newspaper runs a feature article about you. You are receiving a medal for using your skills to make a difference in some area of importance to you. How would the article read?

The *Hometown Gazette* is pleased to award this month's Medal of Accomplishment to (your name) _____ for making a difference in...

_____

_____.

"It really came naturally for me," our medalist states. "All I did was...

_____

_____

_____."

See, I have chosen Bezalel son of Uri, the son of Hur, of the tribe of Judah, 3 and I have filled him with the Spirit of God, with skill, ability and knowledge in all kinds of crafts— 4 to make artistic designs for work in gold, silver and bronze, 5 to cut and set stones, to work in wood, and to engage in all kinds of craftsmanship. 6 Moreover, I have appointed Oholiab son of Ahisamach, of the tribe of Dan, to help him. Also I have given skill to all the craftsmen to make everything I have commanded you.
—Exodus 31:2-6

Delight yourself in the LORD and he will give you the desires of your heart.
—Psalm 37:4

It is God who works in you to will and to act according to his good purpose.
—Philippians 2:13

BIBLE TEXT

See, I have chosen Bezalel son of Uri, the son of Hur, of the tribe of Judah, 3 and I have filled him with the Spirit of God, with skill, ability and knowledge in all kinds of crafts— 4 to make artistic designs for work in gold, silver and bronze, 5 to cut and set stones, to work in wood, and to engage in all kinds of craftsmanship. 6 Moreover, I have appointed Oholiab son of Ahisamach, of the tribe of Dan, to help him. Also I have given skill to all the craftsmen to make everything I have commanded you.
—Exodus 31:2-6

Delight yourself in the LORD and he will give you the desires of your heart.
—Psalm 37:4

It is God who works in you to will and to act according to his good purpose.
—Philippians 2:13

Interactive Page 2

COULD I DO THAT?

Recall a time when you have felt OVERWHELMED by something you were asked to do. Perhaps it was a term paper in your most difficult subject at school, a family member's unrealistic expectation, or a beyond-your-level-of-expertise job responsibility.

• *What was the circumstance? How did you cope?*

Contrast that circumstance with a time when you were CONFIDENT of your competence to do a task.

• *What happened? How were your feelings different?*
• *In each circumstance above, how important was the task to you? How did the importance of the task impact your feelings?*

KEY CONCEPTS
on Heart-Desires and Abilities

#1 God provides _____ _____ toward the work He would have us do.
#2 God both _____ and _____ the desires of our hearts.
#3 Our _____ are gifts from God.
#4 God builds teams of people with _____ _____.

THE VALUE OF TEAMWORK

Think once more about the overwhelming experience you listed above.

• *Could assistance from someone else have enabled you to do the task more comfortably? How could someone have helped?*
• *What skills would that person have needed?*
• *If you had placed either more or less importance on the task, would that have changed your experience? Why, or why not? If so, how?*

'Sure, I Enjoyed That!'
Look back at the circumstance in which you felt confident and competent. List the abilities you used in performing the task:

•

•

•

•

• *Now, think of a cause that is important to you. Could those same abilities be used to make a difference? Why, or why not?*
• *If yes, what would it take to get started?*

IN OTHER WORDS...

Marge Caldwell describes her joy in doing work God has prepared for her. She writes, "I had the eerie feeling you get when you know God is up to something, and you're vitally involved!"
—Marge Caldwell, *Speak Out with Marge*

Our Hearts point us to the "Why?" and "Where?" of serving. Our Abilities determine the "How?" we serve.

Knowing Adam became a privilege for me. . . Who can spend a few hours each day with a man who gives you all his confidence and trust? Isn't that what joy is?
—Henri Nouwen, *Can You Drink the Cup?*

Take Home Page

LOOKING OUTWARD: MY HEART CAUSES

Prayerfully consider the questions below. Assume that it is impossible for you to fail. Consider not only church-related issues, but also concerns affecting your family, work, community or other circles of influence.

• *Ten years from now, I'd like to look back and see that I'd made a difference in ...*

• *What topic would keep you up talking late into the night (if you are a morning person) or cause you to awaken early in the morning (if you are a night owl)?*

• *What needs tug hardest on your heart or frustrate you most when they're not met?*

LOOKING INWARD: MY HEART—MOTIVATIONS

Listed below are actions that describe common motivations of the heart. Choose your three strongest motivations, then see if you can rank the priority of all the listed actions from 1 to 15.

___ ACQUIRE/POSSESS—Shopping, obtaining; finding the best value

___ DESIGN/DEVELOP—Starting something new; making something from nothing

___ EXCEL—Making my team the best; attaining the highest standard

___ FOLLOW THE RULES—Operating by policies and procedures

___ IMPROVE—Improving something that someone else has started

___ INFLUENCE—Converting people to my views; shaping attitudes

___ LEAD/BE IN CHARGE—Leading, supervising, setting policy

___ ORGANIZE—Bringing order out of chaos; organizing something already started

___ OPERATE/MAINTAIN—Efficiently maintaining something already organized

___ PERFORM—Being on stage, in the limelight

___ PERSEVERE—Persisting until the project or task is finished

___ PIONEER—Trying out new concepts; risking failure when necessary

___ PREVAIL—Championing right, opposing wrong; overcoming injustice

___ REPAIR—Fixing what is broken or changing what is out of date

___ SERVE/HELP—Assisting others in their responsibility; helping others succeed

Remember, ALL heart-motives are God-given, to be used for His glory. There are no right or wrong motives, only right motives used correctly or incorrectly.

Take Home Page TRUTH

continued

THE DIAGNOSIS? I DUNNO!

Some people are readily aware of their heart-desires and abilities; others struggle to identify either or both. If listing your heart-causes, heart-motivations or abilities was difficult for you, this exercise may help—

Instructions: Expand the exercise below onto a blank sheet of paper for more space to write. Take some time to reflect over life accomplishments in each time span which (1) were especially meaningful to you, (2) you enjoyed doing, (3) seemed to come very easily and naturally and (4) you believe you did well. In the first column, list the specific accomplishment. In the center column, use action terms to describe how you did it. Finally, analyze what about it was enjoyable. When you have listed three or four items for each time span, look for patterns of causes, motivations, and abilities.

What I Did During My...	How I Did It	Why I Enjoyed It
Early childhood		
Middle school years		
Teens/senior high years		
College years/early 20s		
Mid-20s / mid-30s		
Late-30s to present		

MY GOD-GIVEN ABILITIES

Listed below are categories of specialized skills, aptitudes, and talents. Check all that you do reasonably well, then circle your top three.

— ARTISTIC—conceptualize, picture, draw, paint, photograph
— CLASSIFYING—systemize and file for easy retrieval
— COMPOSING—write music or lyrics
— CONSTRUCTION—carpentry, plumbing, electrical, masonry, etc.
— COUNSELING—listen, encourage and guide with sensitivity
— COUNTING—work with numbers, data or money
— CRAFTS—create objects from fabric, wood, paint, metals, odds and ends
— DECORATING—beautify a setting for a special event
— EDITING—proofread or rewrite
— ELECTRONICS—knowledge/aptitude for computers, other "gadgets"
— EVALUATING—analyze data and draw conclusions
— FEEDING—plan and prepare meals for large or small groups
— GRAPHICS—lay out, design, create visual displays or banners
— INTERVIEWING—discover what others are really like
— LANDSCAPING—garden and work with plants
— LANGUAGES—speak and/or write (what?)
— MANAGING—supervise people to accomplish a task; coordinate details
— MECHANICAL OPERATING—operate equipment, tools or machinery
— MUSICAL—sing or play a musical instrument
— PERFORMING—perform, act, dance, speak, create illusions
— PLANNING—strategize, design and organize programs and events
— PROMOTING—advertise or promote events and activities
— PUBLIC RELATIONS—handle complaints with care and courtesy
— RECALL—remember or recall names and faces
— RECRUITING—enlist and motivate people to get involved
— REPAIRING—fix, restore, maintain
— RESEARCHING—read, gather information, collect data
— RESOURCEFUL—search out and find inexpensive materials or resources
— TEACHING—explain, demonstrate, train, tutor
— WELCOMING—convey warmth, develop rapport, comfort
— WRITING—write articles, letters, books
— OTHER? _____

Session 5

Yes,
THAT WOULD BE ME

What does it mean to be part of the "in crowd" these days?

Segments of society—in various eras—tend to value certain personal styles above others. An individual with an insatiable need to achieve is esteemed in executive circles. An outgoing, gregarious personality makes it in sales positions. A logical and analytical person thrills the academic world.

But society's applause changes with the current vogue. Guys shunned as "computer nerds" in the 1970s are today's "techno-heroes." Gals whom previous generations deemed "unladylike" are today's sports medalists.

Clearly, society's yardstick for measuring personal worth is constantly changing.

With these and many other confusing messages, we lose track of God's design in our lives. We may begin to devalue ourselves—or, on the flip side—become overly impressed with our own importance (depending on who is telling us just how great we are).

God, on the other hand, doesn't change His view of our worth. We are His creation, priceless in His sight . . . always. We don't serve in order to become valuable; we serve because we *are* valuable. Our personal styles are part of God's intentional design on our lives. Knowing our own styles helps us to be more individually effective. Appreciating each other's styles maximizes cooperation and minimizes conflict. Each of our styles is important to God's work, because we're all living in the "inner circle" of the Kingdom.

SESSION AIM

To help single adults identify and value their own personal styles as well as applaud different and/or complementary styles in others.

WHAT'S IT ALL ABOUT?

As you move through your session, keep in mind these Key Concepts you'll be conveying to your group members:

• God's design on our lives was in place even before we were born.
• The same personal style may be used for good or for evil.
• Our personal styles affect how we carry out our ministries.
• There are no right or wrong personal styles.

BIBLE REFERENCES:

Psalm 139:13-16
Galatians 1:13-14
John 11:5; 12:1-3

65

Your 'Short Course' Set-Up...

1—Let's Get Started
(5-10 minutes)

Ask everyone to recall someone they admire, whose behavior they would like to imitate. Discuss:

• *What is it about this person's nature that you admire?*
• *Is this person's disposition very much like—or very different—from your own?*

Make the point that sometimes we are drawn to people who are much like ourselves, who can serve as role models to help us grow toward maturity. Others who hold a special attraction are people who are opposite from us in many ways, who can balance our weaknesses with their strengths, and vice versa. This week's lesson examines "personal styles." It will help us appreciate our own ways of being and learn to celebrate our differences.

2—Looking to the Word
(15 minutes)

Follow the teaching outline on pages 70-72. Cover the Introduction, Key Concepts and Conclusion.

3—Applying It to My Life
(5-10 minutes)

Needed: The "Personal Style Inventory" handout, colored markers.

As soon as you complete your presentation, distribute the "Personal Style Inventory" handout on pages 73-74 and offer these instructions:

1. Work quickly. Check your strongest tendency. Answer according to your preference, without regard for others' expectations, restrictions, or consequences. In other words—not what your mother or your teacher or your best friend or your worst enemy says you should be—but who you really are!

2. If your response to a question is an absolute 50-50 depending upon circumstances, check both columns—but avoid doing so if at all possible. If you can give a 60% response, check that column alone.

3. When you have completed the questions, total your checks at the bottom of each column.

4. Color your totals on the corresponding columns of each profile's graph.

When all group members have colored in their graphs, give the following words to complete the graphs:

Profile 1— S = Structured, F = Flexible
Profile 2— P = People, T = Task
Profile 3—F = Factual, C = Conceptual
Profile 4—T = Thinking, F = Feeling

5. Circle your greater strengths on each profile, then read "Understanding Personal Style Scores."

6. Discuss with one or two other people whether the descriptions of your primary strengths seem to fit.

4—Taking the Next Step
(5 minutes)

Needed: Interactive Page #1, pencils.

Refer everyone to the exercise on Interactive Page #1 titled "Casting By Style." Ask people to select one character and mark which of the four contrasting descriptions better describes that character. discuss:

• *In light of your own personal style inventory, can you guess where the character might fit on two or more of the profiles?*
• *What are your insights on the importance of your own personal style?*

5—Let's Wrap It Up
(5 minutes)

1. Make your group's announcements and distribute the Take Home Page.
2. Close in prayer.

When You Have More Time...
(How to Use This Material in 60-90 Minutes)
Example: Small Groups at Home

1—Let's Get Started
(20-30 minutes)

Option 1: Animal Answers
Needed: Interactive Page #2.

Begin with the exercise titled "Critter Likeness," on Interactive Page #2. Have partners or small groups explain their responses, and then say: Just as God creates different behaviors in the animal kingdom, He has also created unlimited diversity in people's natures. Today's lesson examines personal style. We will see that God designs us with a variety of personalities.

Option 2: Walking My Pet Peeve
Ask everyone to share their pet peeves within a small group by completing this sentence:

"It really drives me crazy when people _____ because _____."

After some discussion, point out that our personal styles can be a source of conflict. The person who is always late drives the punctual person up the wall. The person who enjoys debate annoys a peacemaker. Today we'll look at God's plan for all our personal styles and see how we can work together for His glory.

2—Looking to the Word
(20-30 minutes)

Present the material found in "Presenting What the Bible Has to Say," on Pages 70-72.

3—Applying It to My Life
(30-40 minutes)

Needed: The "Personal Style Inventory" handout, colored markers.

As soon as you complete you presentation, distribute the "Personal Style Inventory" handout on pages 73-74 and offer the instructions given on page 66, step 3.

4—Taking the Next Step
(30 minutes)

Needed: Interactive Page #2.

1. Call attention to "Critter Savvy" on Interactive Page #2. Share your own "critter-likeness" response. Where would you refer it? (Maybe the poodle would be a doggie party planner; the buffalo, a professor of history.)
2. Have everyone complete the exercise—regarding both the critter and themselves—then discuss their responses.

5—Let's Wrap It Up
(5-10 minutes)

Needed: Take Home Page.

1. Make your group's announcements at this time.
2. Hand out the Take Home Page.
3. Encourage everyone to use "Proverbial Ideas and Prayers" as a devotional guide during the coming week.

Extending The Learning...
(How to Use This Material in Two Hours)
Example: Extended Week-Night Program

1—Let's Get Started
(5-10 minutes)

Option 1: Bingo! Icebreaker
Needed: Game cards and pencils.

In advance, prepare a game card with 25 squares (5 across, 5 down). Fill the squares with the following:

Is Impulsive	Seldom Plans
Focuses on Facts	Is a Thinker
Dislikes Schedules	Has a Cat
Is a Movie Buff	Is Organized
Cries at Movies	Is Talkative
Lives for "Now"	Likes variety
Watches the Soaps	Has a Dog
Owns a Bird	Finishes Everything
Acts first, thinks later	Is a Doer
Reads Mysteries	An Exercise Junkie
Dislikes Interruptions	Is a Dreamer
Thinks first, acts later	Is Organized

Distribute the cards and instruct everyone to find people to initial the descriptions that fit them. After a few minutes, call "Stop." Form groups of four to five people who are standing near each other. Ask:

•*Were you surprised by the people who fit some of the categories on your card? Why, or why not?*

Option 2: My Way Is Better
Needed: Slips of paper and a container.

In advance, prepare three to five sets of separate slips containing one of the following numbered words or phrases:

1. Focuses on Facts	1. Dreams of Possibilities
2. Argumentative	2. Peacemaker
3. Premeditating	3. Impulsive
4. Analytical	4. Compassionate

Plan so that an approximately equal number of each word/phrase will be drawn. Form groups by matching numbers. Have those with the same words confer about the strengths of that personality trait, then debate which is better with their opposite characteristic. Encourage a lively and fun exchange.

Make the transition to your Bible presentation by saying: Debates are fun, but such disagreements in real life can be damaging. Today we'll consider the value of each person's strengths. We'll learn to improve our relationships at home, at work and in ministry by understanding our differences.

2—Looking to the Word
(20-25 minutes)

Present the Introduction, Key Concepts and Conclusion on pages 70-72.

3—Applying It to My Life
(20-25 minutes)

Needed: The "Personal Style Inventory" handout, colored markers.

Distribute the "Personal Style Inventory" handout on pages 73-74 and offer the instructions given on Page 66, step 3.

4—Taking the Next Step
(10-20 minutes)

Needed: Overhead projector, transparencies made in advance.

Put two completed profile graphs on an overhead projector or other large media (perhaps these would be yours and a friend's). Use a different color for each person. Circle the four greater strengths of both people at the bottom of their graphs and display both sets of graphs simultaneously. Call for discussion:

•*Based on the graphs, in what kinds of situations would each individual excel?*
•*What challenges or potential problems could you see for each individual?*

After the strengths and challenges have been discussed, disclose the identities represented by each graph. Do this exercise one or more times, as your time permits.

5—Let's Wrap It Up
(5 minutes)

Close with a prayer that each person will come to know, celebrate, and effectively use his or her personal style.

My Personal Game Plan

STEP 1   Time: _____ minutes.

Materials Needed:

Activities Summary:

STEP 2   Time: _____ minutes.

Materials Needed:

Activities Summary:

STEP 3   Time: _____ minutes.

Materials Needed:

Activities Summary:

STEP 4   Time: _____ minutes.

Materials Needed:

Activities Summary:

STEP 5   Time: _____ minutes.

Materials Needed:

Activities Summary:

Just for You
Teacher's Devotional

Someone has suggested that God does not say, "I love you if . . ." but "I love you." Period!

Paul tells us, "I am convinced that neither death nor life, neither angels nor demons, neither the present nor the future, nor any powers, neither height nor depth, nor anything else in all creation, will be able to separate us from the love of God that is in Christ Jesus our Lord" (Rom 8:38-39).

"Personal worth," states Betty Nethery, "is God's gift to us. We don't earn it like Brownie points, and we can't win it through our performance."*

Are you convinced of God's love for you? Just as you are? "Warts and all"?

As you prepare this week's lesson, take time to thank God for who He created you to be. Thank Him for your personal style. Thank Him for each strength He has given you. Thank Him for loving you when you succeed—and when you fail. Thank Him for loving you enough to make you His child.

All of this is simply to say: you yourself must internalize this week's concepts. As you become aware of your personal style, you can use that knowledge to increase your love for people and to help them move into areas of ministry in which they'll be successful. Isn't that the very definition of ministry?

—*Lana Wilkinson*

*Betty Nethery and Beverly Bush Smith, *Uniquely You* (Wheaton: Tyndale House Publishers, Inc., 1984).

MY GOALS FOR THIS SESSION:

- TO HELP SINGLE ADULTS
  _____
  _____
  _____

- TO HELP SINGLE ADULTS
  _____
  _____
  _____

- TO HELP SINGLE ADULTS
  _____
  _____
  _____

- TO HELP SINGLE ADULTS
  _____
  _____
  _____

WHAT I LEARNED FROM READING 'LOOKING TO THE WORD' . . .

Notes and Insights—

69

HINT:

Before you state each Key Concept, ask group members to guess what words will fill in the blanks. For your competitive folks, ask after Concept 4, "How many guessed all the blanks right?" Give 'em a big "hooray!"

Presenting
What the Bible Has to Say...

Here's your mini-lecture covering the biblical Key Concepts. Try to become familiar with the flow of thoughts, and the outline, in order to present this material with maximum eye contact. Special instructions to you are in bold type. (Note: Have group members refer to the Key Concepts section on their Interactive Page. They may wish to fill in the blanks as you speak.)

Introduction

Begin your presentation by asking a volunteer to read Psalm 139:13-16.

Isn't that exciting? God didn't use a cookie cutter to stamp out robots who would all behave alike. He knit us together in our mother's wombs as unique individuals.

Have you ever knitted, or watched someone knit? They start by deciding what they're going to make. Is it an afghan? a shawl? a sweater? What size will it be? What color? One color, or multicolored? Close knit or loose? Washable or dry clean only? Smooth or nubby? Patterned or plain? If patterned, what pattern?

All of these decisions must be made before the yarn and pattern are chosen. Then the work proceeds, the pattern followed. Purposefully, painstakingly, each stitch is looped and tied. Eventually, in skilled hands, a work of art unfolds.

God purposefully chose what He was going to make each of us to be. He planned every detail. Then He purposefully knit us together in our mother's wombs.

Transition Statement: Our personal styles are part of God's intentional design on our lives. Knowing our own styles helps us to be more individually effective. Appreciating each other's styles maximizes cooperation and minimizes conflict. Each of our styles is important to God's work. Let's look a little deeper into God's design on our lives...

KEY CONCEPT #1:
God's design on our lives was in place even before we were born.

Ask someone to read Galatians 1:13-14.

Paul was obviously a radical guy! Whatever he did, he jumped into it 100%. If he believed something, he took action. Before he became a believer in Christ, he persecuted Christians. He knew what he believed and had the depth of conviction and courage to defend his stand.

When Paul became a believer in Christ, did his personal style change? Well, no. He still was a radical guy. He embraced his belief in Christ with the same zeal and commitment that he had previously invested in persecuting the church.

We are all transformed as we follow Christ. Our hearts and minds change. The Holy Spirit produces in us the fruit of love, joy, peace, patience, kindness, goodness, faithfulness, gentleness and self-control. As we mature in our faith, we cease sinful behaviors. But our personal styles—purposefully created—essentially remain unchanged. Because of this...

KEY CONCEPT #2:
The same personal style may be used for good or for evil.

Ask a volunteer to read John 11:5; 12:1-3.

Mary, Martha, and Lazarus were Jesus' close friends. Martha's house was a place where He was comfortable just hanging out.

Here it is party time. Jesus is a local celebrity. Everybody in Bethany knows that Jesus has raised Lazarus from the dead. Now these three close friends throw a bash in His honor.

In this snapshot we learn about the personal styles of Jesus' friends. Martha is doing her practical, hands-on thing, serving food to Jesus and the other guests. Lazarus

is just hanging out with Jesus. His claim to fame was the fact that Jesus had raised him from the dead, but we don't hear that Lazarus set out to tell the world what Jesus had done. Apparently he was a quiet and reserved guy.

Then there was Mary, the demonstrative one. In another passage she had sat at Jesus' feet, hanging on His every word. Now she unabashedly pours expensive perfume on his feet, takes down her hair and wipes his feet with it (not at all a socially appropriate gesture!).*

Here are three close friends, each ministering to Jesus in his or her own way. From this passage we draw two very important principles:

KEY CONCEPT #3:
Our personal styles affect how we carry out our ministries.

I won't ask for a show of hands—but do you ever wish you were just like someone else? Maybe more outgoing? better organized? more tactful? better at confronting? more playful?

(Pause a moment for reflection.)

On the other hand, do you ever wish other people were more like you? Do some people who are very different from you just drive you nuts? (Hey! No finger-pointing allowed!)

Today's study examines personal styles. Our basic temperaments, influenced by our environments, become our personal styles. Our styles of doing things can be modified or flavored, but essentially remain unchanged throughout life.

God designs personalities to behave differently. *When we serve according to His design, our work comes easily and naturally for us.* We are effective, fulfilled, and productive in our efforts.

Understanding personal styles improves our relationships, too. We can learn to work together effectively at home, with friends, at work and in ministry. We can rejoice in our own natural way of being and appreciate each other's differences.

Illustration. Sally is bold and outgoing, the life of the party. Sue is reserved and quiet, a great one-on-one friend. Joe is a thinker who carefully weighs all his options before taking action. Ken is an action-first, take charge kind of guy. They serve together on a single adult ministry task force. Each has a heart for single adults. All bring wonderful skills to the team.

Now that they have worked together for a while, they are driving each other crazy. Sally and Ken appear pushy to Joe and Sue—who, in turn, wish Sally and Ken would stop analyzing everything and "just do it"!

•*Have you ever "been there—done that?" in a situation like this? How did you work things out?*

Understanding our own and each other's personal styles can help us avoid conflict and function as productive and cohesive teams.

KEY CONCEPT #4:
There are no right or wrong personal styles.

"Jesus loved Martha and her sister [Mary] and Lazarus." Although personal styles are not in themselves "right" or "wrong," a particular style certainly can be right or wrong for a particular task. God wants His people to succeed in doing His work. Therefore, we need to discover the kinds of service that God created us to do. Acknowledging our personal styles will help lead us to the "right job" where we can make our unique contributions.

Conclusion
As we seek to find where God would have us serve, we look at our unique God-given combinations of . . .

the "What" God shows us through our Spiritual Gifts
the "Want To" enthusiasm of our Driving Force Gifts
the "Where" of our Heart-Causes
the "Why" of our Heart-Motivations
the "Tools" of our Abilities
and the "How" of our Personal Styles.

Each of these elements is part of God's design on our lives. Next week we will conclude our study by exploring how God uses our experiences to expand and fine-tune our effectiveness in serving.

HINT:

Note that the "Personal Style Inventory" and related information on pages 73-74, are additional reproducible pages that can be used in any of the teaching settings.

*William Barclay, The Daily Study Bible Series, *The Gospel of John, Volume 2* (Philadelphia: Westminster Press, 1975 Edition).

GOING DEEPER

The foundation of our personal styles is our basic temperament. Anyone who has siblings or more than one child knows that children arrive with different temperaments. Some are easygoing; some are intense; others take charge. One dad expressed it this way: "We have three children—one of each kind!"

Our basic temperament is then influenced by our environments. Those influences include birth order, family systems, ethnic, geographical, economic, religious and other cultural circumstances. Physical appearance, illness or handicap, encouragement or the lack thereof, education or its absence—these and many other environmental factors flavor our personal styles.

Some people are keenly aware of their personal styles. Others have difficulty sorting out who they were created to be from how their environments have influenced their development. Those adults who have received encouragement and affirmation tend to value their own personal styles. When adults, for one reason or another, have not been affirmed, or when they have suffered abuse or neglect, they often struggle with feelings of inadequacy and may think that their service is of little value.

Note on "Overcoming Environmental Influences." Scripture abounds with examples of environmental influences, both negative and positive. Negative influences include family systems in which parental favoritism fosters sibling rivalries. Isaac and Rebekah played their twins Esau and Jacob against each other (See Gen. 25:27-28). Jacob, in turn, favored Joseph to the extent that his brothers sold him into slavery (Gen. 37).

Such favoritism causes rifts in families. It fosters loss of personal worth, or rebellion—or a combination of the two—in "unfavorite" children. Single adults who have grown up in families that showed favoritism need to understand that God doesn't play favorites. He has purpose for their lives—just the way He created them. If their response to favoritism was rebellion, they also need to know that He will forgive their rebellion. When they turn their lives over to Him, He will give them the affirmation they long to receive.

Single parents need to understand the importance of recognizing and affirming their children's personal styles. Often, single parents grew up in an environment where they never received the gift of affirmation. They just don't know how to give what they have never received. Understanding their own personal styles and identifying the styles of their children can assist in the processes of learning to value themselves and affirm their children.

Positive biblical family influences include Moses, who was rescued from the Nile by Pharaoh's daughter, nursed by his own mother, and given all the advantages of royalty (Exod. 1:22-2:10). Moses' leadership characteristics were developed and affirmed during his childhood and youth. Even with that affirmation, however, Moses was not used by God when he relied upon his own strength. His forceful personal style, apart from God's leadership, resulted in having to run for his life! (See Exodus 2:11-15.)

Single adults need to understand that whatever their personal style, it must be fully submitted to God if they are to be effective in His service. For many adults, the submission issue is a difficult one. It is especially difficult for those adults whose authority figures have been absent, ineffective, or abusive. Many young adults today have serious trust issues with the authority figures in their lives. From parents to politicians, they have seen too many who did not live up to their promises.

EXTRA INFORMATION TO CONSIDER...

Use this handout as your session leader suggests, or take it home with you for review during the week.

Personal Style Inventory

Respond to each question by placing a check in the column representing your stronger tendency.

PROFILE ONE - HOW AM I ORGANIZED?

	Column S	Column F
I like	___stability	___the unexpected
I prefer guidelines to be	___specific	___general
Rules and policies are	___to be closely followed	___to be used as guidelines
I prefer projects with	___routine	___variety
I live and work by	___sticking to a plan	___playing it by ear
I prefer to work with	___one project at a time	___many projects at one time
Close supervision makes me	___more comfortable	___frustrated and nervous
	___**Total Checks Column S**	___**Total Checks Column F**

PROFILE TWO - HOW AM I ENERGIZED?

	Column P	Column T
I am more comfortable	___being with people	___doing things for people
When doing a task, I usually	___focus on relationships	___focus on the goal
I get more excited about	___creating community	___advancing a cause
I accomplish my goals by	___building relationships	___getting the job done
A meeting should be started	___when everyone arrives	___on time
I'm more concerned with	___maintaining the team	___meeting a deadline
I place higher value on	___communication	___action
	___**Total Checks Column P**	___**Total Checks Column T**

PROFILE THREE - HOW DO I RECEIVE & PROCESS INFORMATION?

	Column F	Column C
I would prefer to teach	___facts	___ideas
When taking a test I prefer	___multiple choice questions	___essay questions
I plan for a task	___detailed from the beginning	___concept first, then specifics
When writing a memo I	___list information in careful order	___insert items or use dashes
I would choose to supervise in	___production and distribution	___design and development
I would rather be known to be	___practical	___ingenious
I approach new problems with	___established methods	___creative solutions
	___**Total Checks Column F**	___**Total Checks Column C**

PROFILE FOUR - HOW DO I MAKE DECISIONS?

	Column T	Column F
My choices are based upon	___logic and analysis	___personal values
As a juror, I would tend	___to give justice	___to give mercy
As a Christian, I'm more aware of	___definable benefits	___experience of blessings
I would rather be known as a	___person of reason	___person of compassion
Conflict in the workplace	___is inevitable	___makes me uncomfortable
People would consider me	___impersonal	___sensitive
I believe parents should be more	___firm	___tender
	___**Total Checks Column T**	___**Total Checks Column F**

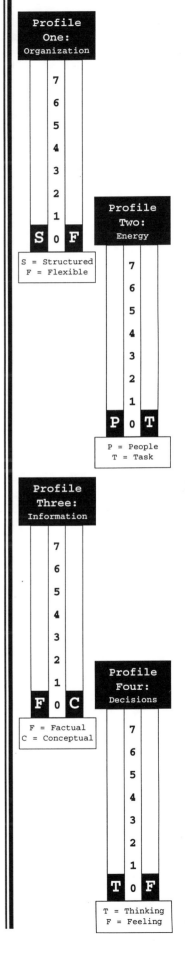

Profile One: Organization

7 6 5 4 3 2 1

S 0 **F**

S = Structured
F = Flexible

Profile Two: Energy

7 6 5 4 3 2 1

P 0 **T**

P = People
T = Task

Profile Three: Information

7 6 5 4 3 2 1

F 0 **C**

F = Factual
C = Conceptual

Profile Four: Decisions

7 6 5 4 3 2 1

T 0 **F**

T = Thinking
F = Feeling

Color both columns on each Profile up to the numbers representing your scores. Wait for instructions, then complete the blank words at the bottom of each profile. Circle the word which represents your greater strength on each profile.

Do the descriptions fit how you see yourself? How you are seen by others who know you well?

The following descriptions are most true for those scoring 5 or higher on a particular strength.

PROFILE ONE: How Am I Organized?
Do you need more structure or more flexibility where you serve?

STRUCTURED	FLEXIBLE
Decisive, planned, self-regimented	Curious, spontaneous, adaptable
Wants to be right	Wants to be open
"Plan the work and work the plan"	Dislikes working on a schedule
Enjoys bringing completion to projects	Can leave projects open for changes

PROFILE TWO: How Am I Energized?
Are you energized more by performing tasks or by being with people?

TASK-ORIENTED	PEOPLE-ORIENTED
Focuses upon the "inside" world — concepts, ideas, abstractions	Focuses upon the "outside" world — people and things
Tends to like quiet time\dislike interruptions	Tends to like action and variety
To know what he's thinking, you must ask	To know what he's thinking, just listen!

PROFILE THREE: How Do I Receive and Process Information?
Do you deal more with ideas and possibilities (concepts) or with hard evidence (facts)?

CONCEPTUAL	FACTUAL
Trusts hunches and takes leaps of faith	Uses sensory information
Is concerned with the meaning of things	The real is seen and touched,
Focuses on possibilities and relationships	Focuses on the real, useful concrete, factual
Anchored more in the future	Anchored more in the present
Work is 95% inspiration, 5% perspiration	Work is 95% perspiration, 5% inspiration

PROFILE FOUR: How Do I Make Decisions?
Are your decisions influenced more by emotion (feeling) or by intellect (thinking)?

FEELING	THINKING
The heart is more important	The head is more important
If it is "good," it has worth and value to people	If it is "good," it is logical and objective
Tactfully and subjectively asks, "How will people respond?"	Impersonally weighs pros and cons
Likes pleasing people in small ways	Pays little attention to people's wishes
Looks at the value of something/someone	Looks at what something/someone is

Key Principles to Remember:

1. You will be most comfortable when the place where you serve relies upon your greater strengths.

2. Your degree of discomfort will increase dramatically if you are serving in an area that leans heavily upon an ability where you scored 2 or less.

3. You can choose to use your lesser strength, even if your score is zero; however, you will be most effective and fulfilled when serving in an area that relies upon a combination of your greater strengths.

CHARACTERS WE KNOW

1. What is your favorite television show?
2. Name three of the show's characters:

-
-
-

3. Think about each character's personality. How does he or she contribute to the comedy, action, or drama of the show?

KEY CONCEPTS
on God's Design

#1 God's design on our lives was _____ even _____ we were born.

#2 The same personal style may be used for_____ _____ or for _____.

#3 Our personal styles affect how we _____ _____ our _____.

#4 There are no _____ or _____ personal styles.

CASTING BY STYLE

Select one of the characters you named from your favorite television show. Consider the contrasting descriptions below. Does that character's personal style appear to be more . . .

___Stable and steady	or	___Spontaneous and adaptable?
___Relationship and team oriented	or	___Goal and project oriented?
___Practical and detail focused	or	___Creative and possibility focused?
___Analytic and impersonal	or	___Compassionate and sensitive?

1. How important is the character's personal style to the show? Stated differently, if his or her style were the opposite in one or more of the above descriptions, what impact would it make on your enjoyment of the character? Of the show? Where do you think this character might fit on today's Personal Style graphs?

2. Let's get back to real life. How important is your own personal style? How does it impact you in your family, your circle of friends, your field of employment, your community and your church?

BIBLE TEXT

For you created my inmost being; you knit me together in my mother's womb. 14 I praise you because I am fearfully and wonderfully made; your works are wonderful, I know that full well. 15 My frame was not hidden from you when I was made in the secret place. When I was woven together in the depths of the earth, 16 your eyes saw my unformed body. All the days ordained for me were written in your book before one of them came to be.
—**Psalm 139:13-16**

Jesus loved Martha and her sister and Lazarus…
1 Six days before the Passover, Jesus arrived at Bethany, where Lazarus lived, whom Jesus had raised from the dead. 2 Here a dinner was given in Jesus' honor. Martha served, while Lazarus was among those reclining at the table with him. 3 Then Mary took about a pint of pure nard, an expensive perfume; she poured it on Jesus' feet and wiped his feet with her hair. And the house was filled with the fragrance of the perfume.
—**John 11:512:1-3**

For you have heard of my previous way of life in Judaism, how intensely I persecuted the church of God and tried to destroy it. 14 I was advancing in Judaism beyond many Jews of my own age and was extremely zealous for the traditions of my fathers.
—**Galatians 1:13-14**

For you created my inmost being; you knit me together in my mother's womb. 14 I praise you because I am fearfully and wonderfully made; your works are wonderful, I know that full well. 15 My frame was not hidden from you when I was made in the secret place. When I was woven together in the depths of the earth, 16 your eyes saw my unformed body. All the days ordained for me were written in your book before one of them came to be.
—Psalm 139:13-16

Jesus loved Martha and her sister and Lazarus… 1 Six days before the Passover, Jesus arrived at Bethany, where Lazarus lived, whom Jesus had raised from the dead. 2 Here a dinner was given in Jesus' honor. Martha served, while Lazarus was among those reclining at the table with him. 3 Then Mary took about a pint of pure nard, an expensive perfume; she poured it on Jesus' feet and wiped his feet with her hair. And the house was filled with the fragrance of the perfume.
—John 11:512:1-3

For you have heard of my previous way of life in Judaism, how intensely I persecuted the church of God and tried to destroy it. 14 I was advancing in Judaism beyond many Jews of my own age and was extremely zealous for the traditions of my fathers.
—Galatians 1:13-14

CRITTER LIKENESS
Personal styles have been categorized in many different ways. Gary Smalley and John Trent's popular inventory describes four personality types as:

___ **Otter** (who is very social and likes to play),
___ **Beaver** (the hard worker who focuses on a task),
___ **Lion** (the take-charge leader, king-or-queen of the jungle) and
___ **Golden Retriever** (who just loves and wants to please everybody).*

•*If you were to select an animal whose personality is much like yours, what would it be, and why?*

KEY CONCEPTS
on God's Design

#1 God's design on our lives was _____ even _____ we were born.
#2 The same personal style may be used for_____ or for _____.
#3 Our personal styles affect how we _____ _____ our _____.
#4 There are no _____ or _____ personal styles.

CRITTER-SAAVY
Think for a moment about the animal you have chosen to relate to your personal style. If you were a "critter employment agency," to what kinds of jobs would you refer that animal?

•*How would that work fit who God designed it to be? Would it enjoy the job?*
•*Now, reflect on your own natural way of being. If you were a ministry employment agency, where would you refer a person such as yourself? Where would you fit? What would you enjoy?*
•*Are you currently serving in such an area? If not, why not?*

TIME FOR A RESPONSE

Write Your Job Description

In the spaces below, jot some of your thoughts and ideas.

• *As you seek to understand your personal style, reread "Understanding Personal Style Scores." Do you relate to the description of your predominate strengths?*

• *Focus on the descriptions of your strengths. What work in your church would capitalize on your personality type? Could it be done in an existing ministry, or might the Lord be leading you to expand an existing ministry? or initiate a new one?*

• *Recalling the previous weeks' studies, where do you think your spiritual gifts, heart, and abilities may be leading you to serve?*

• *Assuming there are others who share your heart for a ministry, what strengths (of personal style, spiritual gifts, and heart) would be helpful for those who might serve as a team with you to carry out this ministry?*

• *Can you identify people in your circle of acquaintance who have those strengths?*

LOOKING AHEAD—

Someone has said, "Experience is what you get when you're looking for something else." Isn't that true? So far, we have examined our . . .

Spiritual gifts
Heart causes and motivations
Abilities and
Personal styles.

Next week, we'll turn to how our

Experiences

impact our service. We'll attempt to answer: *How does God use our experiences—even our blunders and bruises—in His work?*

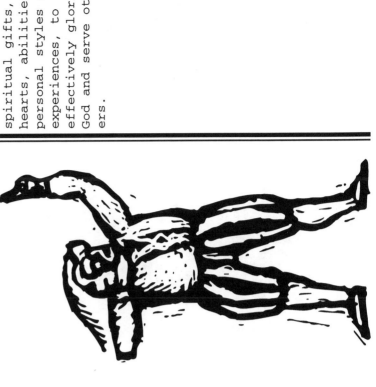

IN OTHER WORDS...

The surest way to find yourself is to lose yourself in something bigger than yourself! I love God's mathematics: Joy adds and multiplies as you divide it with others.

—Mary Crowley, *You Can Too*

Our personal style affects our behavior but does not excuse it. We are responsible for the stewardship of our spiritual gifts, hearts, abilities, personal styles and experiences, to effectively glorify God and serve others.

Take Home Page MARCH

continued

DAILY READINGS AND REFLECTIONS
Proverbial Ideas and Prayers

No matter what our personal styles may be, the Book of Proverbs lends practical guidance to personal effectiveness. Meditate on the following Scriptures and suggested prayers this week.

Monday—Read Proverbs 14:12. The importance of seeking God's direction. Dear Lord, I want to seek Your path for my life, rather than lean on my own wisdom or understanding.

Tuesday—Read Proverbs 13:20. The value of spending time with wise friends. Jesus, I know that Your friendships were of great value to You. Help me to find good friends with whom to share my time.

Wednesday—Read Proverbs 12:13-14. Watching what we say as well as what we do. Father, guard my lips and show me whenever my speech is not pleasing to You.

Thursday—Read Proverbs 11:24-25. The attitude and action of generosity. Lord, You are my provider. Please increase my desire and my ability to generously share what You have given me.

Friday—Read Proverbs 11:3. The value of integrity. Father, I want to be a person of integrity. Help me to match my walk with my talk.

Saturday—Read Proverbs 10:12. The ultimate cure for conflict. Holy Spirit, I ask You to produce the fruit of love more abundantly in my life.

PERSONAL STYLE AND RELATIONSHIPS

Ponder and journal your responses to the following questions.

1. In what areas at work, in friend or family relationships, and/or at church, do your greater strengths enable you to function effectively?

2. Are there areas where your personal style contributes to conflict in relationships? If so, where and how?

3. What complementary strengths should you seek in others who join in team projects with you—at work, in ministry, in other group situations?

4. What might be some cautions that relate to your areas of significantly lesser strength?

"HIM" AND "HER" …AND OTHER THINGS

Consider and respond to the following:

1. Do you think that certain personal styles are considered by our society to be "more appropriate" for males? For females? For certain ethnic groups? Economic status? If so, cite examples.

2. How might society's expectations affect one's joy in his or her personal style?

3. Does God have a gender, ethnic, or economic preference? (See Galatians 3:28.)

Session 6

BEEN THERE,
Done That

Life is tough. It has been so since Adam and Eve ate that first forbidden fruit in the Garden of Eden. Clearly, God doesn't promise that He will protect us from all hardship. In fact, Jesus said, "In this world you will have trouble" (John 16:33). We treasure the joyful experiences of God's guidance and protection, and such experiences yield powerful testimonies. Yet we struggle to understand our tough times. When bad things happen to good people, we may wonder: *Where is God in all of this?*

Yet our life experiences—the good and the bad—help us determine the ministry God has for us. Since life's great messages often come through our weaknesses rather than our strengths, we should pay close attention to the difficult times. That is when God can teach us through the "school of hard knocks."

Scripture does promise that God will take all that happens to us and work it for the good. It is not only through His protection, but also through His comfort in difficult times that we learn to rely on Him. And some of our most successful ministries occur as we testify about God's faithfulness in taking us through painful tribulation. For effectiveness in ministry flows through His strength, not our own. As the song "Ordinary People" so eloquently states, "Little becomes much when you place it in the Master's Hand."*

*Danibelle Hall, "Ordinary People" (Birdwing Music/Dannibelle Music/Cherry Lane Music Co., 1977).

SESSION AIM

To help single adults view all of their experiences as preparation for ministry, causing them to rely on His strength in all circumstances.

WHAT'S IT ALL ABOUT?

As you move through your session, keep in mind these Key Concepts you'll be conveying to your group members:

• God uses all of our experiences—even those that hurt—to prepare us for ministry.
• Confidence and joy come from knowing that we are serving according to God's purposes.
• The true test of our service is the fruit we produce.

BIBLE REFERENCES:

2 Corinthians 1:3-4
Romans 8:28
Philippians 1:12
Galatians 5:22-23

79

HINT:

When planning what to present, evaluate your group. Are they folks who have barely begun their journeys and are still struggling with whether they even want to go to higher places? Are they basking comfortably in the Sonlight of the foothills, content to let others do ministry for them? Are some of them in the middle of very painful times? Where are they on their journeys?

1—Let's Get Started
(5-10 minutes)

Option 1: Jesus on Your Donkey
Needed: Interactive Page #1.

Distribute Interactive Page #1, form small groups, and ask everyone to read "Jesus on Your Donkey?" After fielding some responses to the discussion question, make the point that believers today are the "vehicles" God uses to tell others about Himself. Today we conclude our course by examining how our experiences affect our ability to move Jesus' story down the road.

Option 2: Learning by Experience

Form small groups and ask participants to discuss these questions together:

•What is your favorite hobby? Why do you enjoy it? How long have you done it?
•Are you better at this hobby now than when you first started? How did you improve?
•Can you recall a time when you botched it big-time? What did you learn in the process?

Have one of your own stories ready to share as an example. Make it funny, if possible, and tell it in view of this lesson's focus. Maybe you're a skier. You love exercise and snow. Tell about an early crash. How did you improve? Perhaps you almost froze your legs in an unexpected spring storm and learned to dress in layers.

As a transition, make the point that our favorite hobbies are things we choose because of how we're wired. They're different for each person. Sometimes our experiences lead us into the hobby; always our experience fine-tunes our ability to enjoy the hobby. Today we'll look at how our experiences impact our ministries.

2—Looking to the Word
(15 minutes)

Familiarize yourself with pages 84-86 and present the mini-lecture there.

3—Applying It to My Life
(5-10 minutes)

Needed: Interactive Page #1.

As soon as you complete your presentation, direct attention to "What Is Your Donkey?" on the Interactive Page. Ask group members to spend a few minutes silently reflecting and making notes in response to the listed questions. Ask them to remain silent if they finish early. When your allotted time is nearly gone, pray through today's Scriptures. Ask God's comfort for those who are in pain. Thank Him for using "all things" for our good and our "happenings" to advance the Gospel.

4—Taking the Next Step
(5 minutes)

Place the acronym "S.H.A.P.E." on the chalk board and lead the group to complete the blanks, one at a time. Work to get everyone involved. Even those who have missed previous lessons will know "Experiences."

5—Let's Wrap It Up
(5 minutes)

Needed: A music recording: "Ordinary People."

1. Make your group's announcements and then play a recording of the song, "Ordinary People."
2. Close with a prayer that each of your "littles" will become "much" in the Master's hand!
3. Distribute the Take Home Page.

When You Have More Time...

(How to Use This Material in 60-90 Minutes)

Example: Small Groups at Home

1—Let's Get Started
(5-10 minutes)

Option 1: Shoes Made for Walking
Needed: Interactive Page #2.

Refer to the exercise on Interactive Page #2 titled "These Shoes Are Made for Walking." Form groups of four to five people. Ask everyone to read the instructions and then reflect and make notes. After a few minutes, ask participants to share their experiences with their groups.

A fun alternative: As the exercise begins, ask everyone to remove their shoes. Ask them to relate the shoes they are wearing to their life experiences, in light of the questions in the exercise. Do the shoes fit, or would they choose a different pair to describe their lives—and why?

Option 2: Choose a Shoe
Needed: All kinds of shoes.

Collect a variety of shoes, from baby shoes to work boots, women's high heels, ballerina slippers, cowboy boots, sandals, etc. (If you're mechanically inclined, you might include brake shoes, for a laugh.) Ask the group to choose a pair from the assortment that would represent their life experiences—where they have been and are going—then tell a partner which shoes they have chosen and why.

Make the point that each of us brings different life experiences to our present and will have different experiences in our futures. Today we will study how God uses our experiences in ministry.

2—Looking to the Word
(20-25 minutes)

Present "What the Bible Has to Say" on pages 84-86.

3—Applying It to My Life
(20-25 minutes)

Once you complete your presentation, refer to "Hiking Mountains and Valleys" on Interactive Page #2. Ask everyone to take a few minutes to make some notes in response to each of the questions. Form groups of no more than four and ask people to share about their responses and then pray for each other in light of those experiences.

4—Taking the Next Step
(10-20 minutes)

Needed: Take Home Page; note paper and envelopes.

1. Distribute the Take Home Page and have those who know the words to complete the "SHAPE" acronym and state them aloud, giving enough time between statements for everyone to fill in the blanks.

2. Ask participants to take a few moments to think through what they have learned during this study and what action they will take to implement their knowledge. Have them write on the paper some personal ministry involvement goals that can be accomplished within 30 days, then address the envelope to themselves, sealing their goals inside. Collect the envelopes and mail them, as addressed, one month from today.

5—Let's Wrap It Up
(5 minutes)

Needed: Take Home Page.

1. Point to the Take Home Page's "My SHAPE for Service." Encourage the group to pull their own "ministry picture" into view.

2. Optional: Ask everyone to complete "My SHAPE for Service" as homework. Extend the study and have them bring their completed forms back next week, prepared to pray for each others' ministries and to explore together where God may be leading each of them to serve.

3. Make your announcements and close in prayer.

IMPORTANT:

Distribute assessments from previous lessons to any group members who missed those, so those folks can complete this final form on page 96.

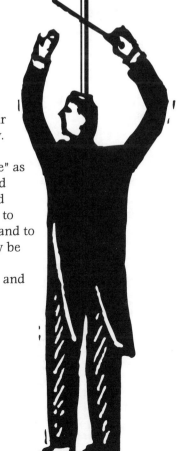

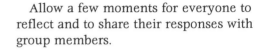

HINT:

Move mountains with the men and women who have completed this study. Help them complete "My SHAPE for Service." If you need to photocopy the assessments they missed in previous sessions, do it; get them to fill out all the assessment forms. Place these folks into service. Take off your shoes; you are standing on Holy Ground!

1—Let's Get Started
(20-30 minutes)

Option 1: Interactive Exercises

Needed: Interactive Pages #1 or #2.

You may use either of the Interactive Page exercises to open your session. With Interactive Page #1, use Step 1 instructions on page 80. With Interactive Page #2, use page 81. (You may also choose other Step 1 options from page 87.)

Option 2: Truth or Fiction?

Form small groups. Ask everyone to think of three experiences to tell about themselves. Two are true, the other is ... well ... a fabrication. Others guess which statement is NOT true. Set the pace with your own experiences. Recall two true stories that might be difficult to believe and one false one that could be true. Have everyone guess which is false, then play the game in their groups.

After all have shared, say, "Did you learn anything new about anyone? Maybe that _____ (a good sport) can tell a bald-faced lie with a straight face?"

As a transition statement, say: "Some of us may not have hard-to-believe experiences, but all of us have experiences that God uses to mold us and influence the way we serve."

2—Looking to the Word
(20 minutes)

Read and become thoroughly familiar with pages 84-86 before presenting this material to your group.

3—Applying It to My Life
(30-40 minutes)

When you're through presenting "Looking to the Word," have everyone gather in small groups and pose this question:

•If you were to name one experience that has impacted your relationship with Christ more than any other, what would that experience be?

Allow a few moments for everyone to reflect and to share their responses with group members.

4—Taking the Next Step
(30-40 minutes)

Needed: Take Home Page.

1. Distribute the Take Home Page and have those who know the words to complete the "SHAPE" acronym and state them aloud, giving enough time between statements for everyone to fill in the blanks.
2. Review and summarize the study by leading the group into the Take Home Page exercise titled "My SHAPE for Service." Encourage everyone to think back through past lessons and pull their responses forward for a thumbnail sketch of their "shape." Distribute missing assessments to any who missed sessions 1-5, and just get people started on the exercise, if your time is running short (they can complete the form at home at their leisure).

5—Let's Wrap It Up
(5-10 minutes)

1. IMPORTANT: Distribute inventories/assessments for any previously-missed sessions. Encourage everyone to complete all inventories they have missed.
2. Close with a prayer that each person will come to appreciate who God has created them to be. Seek His guidance for each to discover what God would have them to do. Pray for the fruit of the Spirit to grow continually more abundant in each life.

My Personal Game Plan

STEP 1   Time: _____ minutes.

Materials Needed:

Activities Summary:

STEP 2   Time: _____ minutes.

Materials Needed:

Activities Summary:

STEP 3   Time: _____ minutes.

Materials Needed:

Activities Summary:

STEP 4   Time: _____ minutes.

Materials Needed:

Activities Summary:

STEP 5   Time: _____ minutes.

Materials Needed:

Activities Summary:

Just for You
Teacher's Devotional

"The leader of the future," states Don Zimmer, "leads in a radically different way, not on what the world values but in the footsteps of the servant leader, Jesus. [Here] the measure is not in what the leader does but in the answer to the question, 'Are the served becoming healthier, freer, wiser, more autonomous and more likely themselves to become servants?' "*

Jesus said, "Remain in me, and I will remain in you. No branch can bear fruit by itself; it must remain in the vine. Neither can you bear fruit unless you remain in me. I am the vine; you are the branches. If a man remains in me and I in him, he will bear much fruit; apart from me you can do nothing...This is to my Father's glory, that you bear much fruit, showing yourselves to be my disciples" (John 15:4-5, 8).

How's your fruit? Does it grow from the Vine or only from your training, abilities, personality and experiences? "You did not choose me," Jesus continued, "but I chose you and appointed you to go and bear fruit—fruit that will last" (John 15:16)

Remember that you are chosen. Be a servant-leader. Enlist others. Equip them. Send them forth. Grow an orchard!

—Lana Wilkinson

*Don Zimmer, "The Leader of the Future is a Servant First," presented September 1997 at Single Adult Pastors Forum, hosted by The Leadership Network at Colorado Springs, Colorado.

MY GOALS FOR THIS SESSION:

- TO HELP SINGLE ADULTS
  _____
  _____
  _____

- TO HELP SINGLE ADULTS
  _____
  _____
  _____

- TO HELP SINGLE ADULTS
  _____
  _____
  _____

- TO HELP SINGLE ADULTS
  _____
  _____
  _____

WHAT I LEARNED FROM READING 'LOOKING TO THE WORD'...

Notes and Insights—

LOOKING TO THE WORD—BEEN THERE, DONE THAT!

Presenting
What the Bible Has to Say...

H ere's your mini-lecture covering the biblical Key Concepts. Try to become familiar with the flow of thoughts, and the outline, in order to present this material with maximum eye contact. Special instructions to you are in bold type. (Note: Have group members refer to the Key Concepts section on their Interactive Page. They may wish to fill in the blanks as you speak.)

Introduction

Matt was excited. College was behind him; an advertising career loomed ahead. He had interviewed for his dream job on Monday. Matt's portfolio was excellent; Mr. Marley had said so. The interview went well. He eagerly awaited the call to pack his bags for the Big Apple.

He was surprised when a letter arrived, saying: "The agency appreciates your interest. Your portfolio shows excellent potential. We regret to inform you, however, that we have hired a more experienced individual. Sincerely yours, Joseph Marley."

"More experienced!" Matt bellowed. "More experienced? This is the sixth job that turned me down because I am not experienced. How am I going to get experience, if nobody will hire me because I have no experience?"

Have you ever been there, done that?

Transition Statement: Our life experiences are important factors in determining our careers—and the ministry God has for us. Since life's great messages often come through our weaknesses rather than our strengths, we should pay close attention to difficult times and what God has taught us through the "school of hard knocks." Today's lesson looks at how God uses *all* of our experiences. We will discover that His work comes with on-the-job training. It's a job called "life."

Option: Before you present the first key concept, ask for a volunteer or two to share their experience with the group related to these questions:

•*Can you think of times when you have been able to comfort someone because of something you have been through? Or: have you received comfort during a difficult time from someone else who'd 'been there, done that'?"*

 **KEY CONCEPT #1:
God uses all our experiences—even those that hurt—to prepare us for ministry.**

When we consider qualifications for work, we think of formal education, apprenticeship, special skills training, and years on the job. Certainly, all these are beneficial in Christian service. But God has an unusual way of empowering the weak. When we choose to follow Him, God takes the "stuff" we learn in life's trenches—both the good and the bad—and uses it for our good and His glory.

Ask a volunteer to read 2 Corinthians 1:3-4.

Have you ever thought about *how* God comforts us in our troubles? Although we would not choose the difficult experiences, it is through those times that God reveals His love and grace. Someone has said: "Prosperity is a great teacher; adversity, a greater teacher." Some of our greatest growth occurs in the wake of adversity.

Think for a moment of people who have experienced great victory through incredibly difficult circumstances. One example is Corrie ten Boom, who survived a World War II Nazi extermination camp. *The Hiding Place,* her incredible story of faith, has touched millions of lives.* Not only did she survive, but she forgave her oppressors. She received God's comfort; she passed it on.

Our painful experiences may not be so dramatic. They may involve broken promises, broken relationships, illness, financial reverses, or the death of loved ones. Yet when these events are submitted to God's healing touch, each of our painful experiences become testimonies He can use in the lives of others.

Ask another volunteer to read Romans 8:28.

Everyone—both believers and unbelievers—experiences problems. But that which should distinguish the suffering of believers from unbelievers is the confidence that our suffering is under the control of an all-powerful and all-loving God. Our suffering has meaning and purpose in God's eternal plan, and He brings (or allows to come into our lives) only that which is for His glory and our good. +

Have someone read Philippians 1:12.

Paul wrote this letter to the Philippians from house arrest in a Roman jail, chained to a Roman guard. Yet Paul could rejoice about what was happening. Why? Because he knew that he was doing what God had called him to do.

Now, think about this just for a minute. We know that Paul had a vision problem. Many of his letters had to be dictated. God gives him the job of spreading the Gospel to the Gentiles, and these Roman guards—Gentiles—have to stay here and listen to him dictate letters about Jesus. Isn't that rich? The entire Roman guard learned about Christ! Thus the Book of Philippians describes Paul's joy in the midst of difficult circumstances.

KEY CONCEPT #2:
Confidence and joy come from knowing that we are serving according to God's purposes.

Read, or have someone read, Galatians 5:22-23.

God gives us Spiritual Gifts, Heart-desires, Abilities, Personal styles and Experiences—all to be used to serve Him. When we submit to His leadership, He guides us in ministry—shows us what to do and gives us the energy to do it, through his Holy Spirit.

Yet we're constantly tempted to minister from our strengths rather than through the strength and guidance of the Holy Spirit. When we serve from the flesh, we produce the fruit of the flesh. Therefore, as we serve, it is important for us to do a frequent "fruit check." Are we ministering in our own strength, or under the leadership of the Holy Spirit?

Look again at the fruit of the Spirit. As you serve, are you behaving in a loving manner? Are you joyful? Are you at peace internally and with those around you? Are you becoming more patient, kind, good, faithful and gentle? Are you better able today to control your tongue and negative behaviors than you were six months or a year ago? Or are you serving from selfish ambition, trying to earn Brownie points, jealous, promoting discord, behaving like children "fighting over the presents"?

KEY CONCEPT #3:
The true test of our service is the fruit we produce.

Too often we are ineffective because we serve in our own strength. We say, "Thanks, God, for saving me. I'll study Your Word—and when I get knowledgeable enough, I'll do Your work."

We fail to comprehend the importance of the trees in the center of the Garden of Eden (Gen. 2:9). The Tree of Life yields the fruit of the Spirit; the Tree of Knowledge of Good and Evil, the fruit of the flesh (Gen. 2:17). Satan tempted Eve not with blatant sin, but with her desire for knowledge (Gen. 3:5-6). He uses the same guise today.

Look up Galatians 5:19. Read it.

Immorality, impurity, rage, drunkenness—these are easily recognizable sins. But Satan tempts committed Christians much more subtly. Our ministries become our idols. We envy those with more resources or bigger ministries. We disguise dissension as doctrinal debate. We act like children, fighting over our presents.

It is time we grew up. Jesus said in John 15:5, "I am the vine; you are the branches. If a man remains in me and I in him, he will bear much fruit; apart from me you can do nothing." Nothing. Zero. Nada. Zilch.

Look in your heart, where no one else can see. What fruit grows there?

*Corrie ten Boom with John and Elizabeth Sherrill, *The Hiding Place*. (Minneapolis: World Wide Publications for the Billy Graham Evangelistic Association, 1971).

+Jerry Bridges, *Trusting God Even When Life Hurts* (Colorado Springs: Navpress, 1988), 32.

HINT:

If your group members are like most single adults, they collectively—and sometimes individually—experience each of the problems faced by Hanna Hurnard's character, Much Afraid. Learn the story well enough to tell it, or simply read the synopsis from the lesson. Ask, "What are some influences that might keep you or others you know from beginning or continuing the journey to the High Places?" Make your own list in addition to the text. After some discussion, ask, "Do you think Christians are more prone to stay in the High Places with the Chief Shepherd or to return to help others in the Valley? What are you more prone to do?" If time permits, call for comment or discussion; otherwise, just ask people to silently reflect on the question.

Conclusion

God has created us with unique combinations of **S**piritual gifts, **H**eart-desires, **A**bilities and **P**ersonal styles. He then fine-tunes us through our **E**xperiences. This becomes our SHAPE for service! As we answer His call to serve and fully yield to His Spirit, our lives are dramatically transformed. We are filled with love, joy, peace, patience, kindness, goodness, faithfulness, gentleness and self-control. We rise above the mundane and natural into the extraordinary and supernatural. We shall never again be the same.

GOING DEEPER

God uses the tools of experiences to chip away our old, selfish natures and transform us to the image of Christ. Sometimes, the tool that He uses is pain.

An Excellent Illustration. Hannah Hurnard's *Hind's Feet on High Places* + + is an allegory about spiritual growth. Its title comes from Habakkuk 3:19: "The LORD God is my strength, and he will make my feet like hinds' feet, and he will make me to walk upon mine high places (KJV)."

The main character, a crippled young woman named Much Afraid, lives in the Valley of Humiliation. She serves the Chief Shepherd and longs to go with Him to the High Places of his Father's Kingdom, the Realm of Love. She hesitates to begin the journey because she is not only crippled, but also afraid of the vulnerability of Love. Her family, the Fearings, hate the Shepherd and want to keep her in the valley. The tale unfolds as she flees with the Chief Shepherd toward the High Places.

The Shepherd first plants the seed of love in her heart. It will grow along her journey. He then gives her two companions to help her climb the steep and difficult places. Their names are Sorrow and Suffering. Together they weather many difficulties. Cousin Pride attempts to talk her out of the climb. They detour through the Desert, Shores of Loneliness, the Valley of Loss. The Chief Shepherd invariably assists whenever they call. Eventually they reach the Healing Streams in the foothills of the Kingdom of Love. Much Afraid's fruit of Love blossoms.

The Chief Shepherd changes Much Afraid's name to Grace and Glory. Her companions Sorrow and Suffering become Joy and Peace. No longer crippled and afraid, Grace and Glory joyfully leaps "with hinds' feet"—like a deer—over the mountains with the Chief Shepherd. She reaches and celebrates the High Places, basking in the beauty of the Kingdom of Love.

One day, looking out from the Kingdom, Grace and Glory realizes that her relatives—Craven Fear, Pride, Bitterness, Resentment, Self-Pity, Aunt Dismal, Gloomy and Spiteful—are still trapped in the valley. They aren't acquainted with the Chief Shepherd. She wants so much for them to know Him and His freedom. She realizes that she and her companions must return to the valley, to share with others the life which they have received. Triumphantly, she returns to rescue her family.

Roadblocks and Challenges. Numerous are the detours that would discourage us from seeking the High Places. Busy schedules, old habits, fear of commitment, lack of understanding—all distract from our journeys toward spiritual maturity. Our first challenge is to begin our journeys; the second, to persevere.

Some of us just want to stay with the Chief Shepherd. We hang out in the foothills or hike to the High Places—but fail to comprehend that, like Jesus, we must serve. Our third challenge is to leave the High Places of our comfort zones and share our freedom in Christ with those still trapped in the valley.

you are here

EXTRA OPTIONS

Pick and Choose any of the following to fit the needs of your group...

Options to Consider...for Step 1

Many Roads, Same Destination—
Select a detailed map of a large city, state, or region. Mark two intersections in the city or two cities in the state or region that are at opposite corners of the map. Run photocopies for everyone in your group. Distribute the maps and a colored crayon or marker to each person. Have "players" try to trace as many different routes as possible to connect the two destinations, without duplicating a road in any of the routes.

   After a few minutes, form groups and have people compare the routes they have marked. Then relate the map to our life's experiences and the destination to Christian service. make the point that each person's experiences are different. Some travel congested freeways; others take the scenic route. Discuss:

   •What kind of road would best describe your own journey so far, and why?

Options to Consider...for Step 3

Melodrama and Pantomime: "Fruitful Antonyms"—This melodrama may be used as a discussion-starter for Step 3. It will require this advanced preparation:
   •Make name placards on letter-sized cards suspended from yarn with the names, "Jane R. Believer," "John Q. Christian," "Satan" (in black lettering) and "God" (in red lettering).

   •Make reversible signs on construction paper or colored card stock in the shape of fruit, with the following pairs of words (Satan's words on one side, God's on the other):
   "Hatred / Love"
   "Misery / Joy"
   "Fighting / Peace"
   "Demanding / Patient"
   "Vicious / Kind"
   "Evil / Good"
   "Fickle / Faithful"
   "Cruel / Gentle"
   "Negligent / Self-Controlled"
   •Make Two audience banners, one reading, "Hiss! Boo!" and the other, "Applause! Hooray!"

   CAST AND SETTING: Four characters, each wearing a name placard. Two audience prompters, each holding one banner. Stage with common props such as chairs, table, flowers, food, magazines.
   JOHN AND JANE: Enter, pause to face audience, smile, bow and point to name placard. Start happily walking hand in hand across the stage. They pause to admire the flowers.

   1. SATAN: Slinks in, faces audience and points to name placard, then hands the fruit "Hatred" to John.
   2. JOHN: Distorts face, crosses arms over chest, with an expression of hatred toward Jane.
   3. AUDIENCE PROMPTER: Waves "Hiss! Boo!" sign. (Leader, give this a big raspberry!)
   4. GOD: Walks confidently in, faces audience and points to name placard, then turns to dismiss Satan with a wave and reverses John's sign to read "Love."
   5. JOHN: Accepts the sign, places it on the table, smiles, opens arms and gives Jane a hug.

++Hannah Hurnard, *Hinds Feet on High Places* (Wheaton: Tyndale House Publishers, Inc., 1975). Don't let this study end as theory to your single adults. Make it come alive in their lives by assisting them in finding areas of service where they can put these principles into practical action. They'll love you for it!
   This moving spiritual growth allegory is available in paperback for $4.95. It makes wonderful reading for yourself or gifts for your ministry leaders.

*"The Hiding Place," © 1975, World Wide Pictures, Inc., distributed by Republic Pictures Home Video.

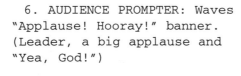

6. AUDIENCE PROMPTER: Waves "Applause! Hooray!" banner. (Leader, a big applause and "Yea, God!")

Steps 1 through 6 are repeated (without pausing to show name placard, of course), alternating signs to Jane and John, who portray the actions of each of the other fruit antonym pairs. Have the characters decide how to portray each set of words. Here are a few ideas:

• With "misery," Jane could sit down, dejected, pouting, ignoring John; then dance around with "joy."
• With "fighting," Jane and John might pantomime an argument, waiving angry fists; then smile, nod and shake hands with "peace."
• With "vicious," John can point and make fun of Jane, bringing her to tears. Illustrate "kind" by encouraging her with a pat on the shoulder, a stroke of her hair and a "you can do it" nod.

John and Jane continue to alternate individual and/or joint portrayals of each pair of actions. When all the fruit have been acted upon, SATAN and GOD move center stage. SATAN stands pridefully with his "Hatred" fruit sign; God is confident but empty-handed. JOHN, JANE and the AUDIENCE PROMPTERS each pick up two signs from the table; two walk to left stage, two to right.

JOHN, JANE and the AUDIENCE PROMPTERS: Holding one sign in either hand, Satan's side forward, say in unison, "Whose fruit are you picking? Fruit of the flesh?"

SATAN: Smiles and holds up "Hatred."

Pause.

GOD: Turns and boldly points finger at Satan, who hands the sign to God, then shrinks away.

JOHN, JANE and the AUDIENCE PROMPTERS: "Or fruit of the Spirit?" (All signs are turned over).

Antonyms in Real Life—If you use "Melodrama and Pantomime," ask participants to think about times when they respond to life's circumstances with the "fruit of the flesh." What are some patterns they see repeating in their own lives? In the lives of other Christians they know? How might they turn those times over to the Lord and experience the fruit of the Spirit instead?

Options to Consider...for Step 4
Experience Charades
Needed: 10 slips of paper; two containers for drawing; a stop watch or watch with a seconds display.

Form two equal-sized teams. Give each group five paper slips. Have each group name five different experiences that God could use to prepare a person for ministry. Place each team's slips in a container and exchange containers. The teams will then take turns drawing and acting out the experiences. Keep score by tallying the total seconds required; maximum time is 60 seconds. The team with the lower score is the winner.

Where Are Your Keys?
Advance Preparation: On five posterboards, recreate the Key Concepts for Sessions one through five. Leave the appropriate blank spaces to be filled in.

Review the previous five weeks Key Concepts. Take the sections one at a time, holding us the posterboards for all to see. Ask for volunteers to state how each blank should be filled in.

Option to Consider...for Step 5
Video Showing—The classic film, "The Hiding Place,"* is available at major video rental stores. Ask each person to reflect about how their victory over a painful circumstance might be used in the work God is calling them to do.

JESUS ON YOUR DONKEY?

The 21st chapter of Matthew records Jesus' triumphal entry into Jerusalem. Jesus told His disciples to go to a village, find a donkey and her colt, and bring them to Him. Jesus said, "If anyone says anything to you, tell him that the Lord needs them, and he will send them right away."

Jesus rode in on the donkey. The crowds were ecstatic. They tossed palm branches and shouted praises (Matt. 21:1-9). Max Lucado, in "The Triumphal Entry," describes his desire to interview the guy who owned that donkey.* The questions Max would like to ask include: "How did you know it was Jesus who needed a donkey?" "Was it hard to give?" "How did it feel . . . ? Were you proud? Were you surprised? Were you annoyed?"

•Can you imagine Jesus riding on your donkey—or your Chevy, or your bike, or your rollerblades? How would you have felt if Jesus were riding on your donkey?

KEY CONCEPTS
on Life Experiences

#1 God uses all of our _____—even those that _____—to prepare us for ministry.

#2 _____ and _____ come from knowing that we are serving according to God's purposes.

#3 The true test of our service is the _____ we produce.

WHAT IS YOUR DONKEY?

Lucado states, "All of us have a donkey. You and I each have something in our lives, which, if given back to God, could, like the donkey, move Jesus and His story further down the road. Maybe you can sing or hug or program a computer or speak Swahili or write a check. Whichever, that's your donkey. Whichever, your donkey belongs to him."

•If experiences were donkeys, what might your donkey be?

For clues, look back at today's Scriptures—
2 Corinthians 1:3-4: *What comfort can you give because God has comforted you in a time of similar trouble?*

Romans 8:28: *In what circumstances is God working for your good?*

Philippians 1:12: *What "happenings" is God using to "advance the Gospel" to you or to others you know?*

Galatians 5:22-23: *What fruit are you producing as you serve? Is the fruit of the Spirit your donkey? Or are you the owner of a mule that is producing fruits of pride, jealousy, selfishness, discord, impurity, etc.?*

•Think back over previous sessions. What else do you have that could move Jesus further down the road?

And we know that in all things God works for the good of those who love him, who have been called according to his purpose.
—Romans 8:28

Praise be to the God and Father of our Lord Jesus Christ, the Father of compassion and the God of all comfort, 4 who comforts us in all our troubles, so that we can comfort those in any trouble with the comfort we ourselves have received from God.
—1 Corinthians 1:3-4

But the fruit of the Spirit is love, joy, peace, patience, kindness, goodness, faithfulness, 23 gentleness and self-control. Against such things there is no law.
—Galatians 5:22-23

Now I want you to know, brothers, that what has happened to me has really served to advance the gospel.
—Philippians 1:12

*Max Lucado, *The Greatest Moments* (Hong Kong: Word Publishing, 1995).

And we know that in all things God works for the good of those who love him, who have been called according to his purpose.
—Romans 8:28

Praise be to the God and Father of our Lord Jesus Christ, the Father of compassion and the God of all comfort, 4 who comforts us in all our troubles, so that we can comfort those in any trouble with the comfort we ourselves have received from God.
—1 Corinthians 1:3-4

But the fruit of the Spirit is love, joy, peace, patience, kindness, goodness, faithfulness, 23 gentleness and self-control. Against such things there is no law.
—Galatians 5:22-23

Now I want you to know, brothers, that what has happened to me has really served to advance the gospel.
—Philippians 1:12

THESE SHOES ARE MADE FOR WALKING

Compare your life experiences to a pair of shoes. Where have the shoes been? Where are they going? Are they laced tight or open? Colorful or plain? Rugged or formal? Scuffed or polished? Leather or canvas?

•*If your life were a pair of shoes, what kind of shoes would it be, and why?*

KEY CONCEPTS
on Life Experiences

#1 God uses all of our _____—even those that _____—to prepare us for ministry.

#2 _____ and _____ come from knowing that we are serving according to God's purposes.

#3 The true test of our service is the _____ we produce.

HIKING MOUNTAINS AND VALLEYS

Put yourself in hiking boots. You've got your backpack and tent on your shoulders. You've been traveling upward for a while. Now you're resting for a moment, looking back over the climb you've just made.

Reread each of the Scripture passages from today's lesson. Describe how you you experienced the truth of these Scriptures.

2 Corinthians 1:3-4: *How have you given or received comfort because God has comforted you or your comfort-giver in a time of similar trouble?*

Romans 8:28: *In what circumstances do you see God working for your good and/or for the good of others who love Him?*

Philippians 1:12: *Has God used, or is He using, difficulties to "advance the gospel" to you or to others you know? What are those "happenings"?*

Galatians 5:22-23: *What fruit are you producing as you serve? Is the fruit of the Spirit becoming more evident in your life—or are you producing fleshly fruit such as jealousy, selfishness, discord or impurity?*

'COMFORT' PRAYER

Dear Heavenly Father, I am so grateful for the comfort You give me during my troublesome times. Thank You for working through all the experiences of my life—even my mistakes, even those experiences that hurt—for my good. Lord, I want to comfort others with the comfort You have given me. I want to know the confidence and joy that flows from knowing Your purpose for me. I long for more fruit of Your Spirit in my life. Show me Your place for my service and help me to rely on Your strength as I serve. Amen.

My S.H.A.P.E. for Service
"Pulling It Together!"

Name_____

Date of Workshop:_____

Based upon the profiles I have completed and my current level of understanding, I believe the information below represents my "S.H.A.P.E."

Spiritual Gifts

Top Four	Score
_____	_____
_____	_____
_____	_____
_____	_____

"Driving Force" Gift:

_____

Heart

Causes:

_____

_____

_____

_____

Motivations (Rank):

1. _____
2. _____
3. _____

Abilities

I'm best at:

_____

_____

_____

_____

I also can:

_____

_____

Personal Style

Profile One: Organization	Profile Two: Energy	Profile Three: Information	Profile Four: Decisions
7	7	7	7
6	6	6	6
5	5	5	5
4	4	4	4
3	3	3	3
2	2	2	2
1	1	1	1
S o **F**	**P** o **T**	**F** o **C**	**T** o **F**
S = Structured F = Flexible	P = People T = Task	F = Factual C = Conceptual	T = Thinking F = Feeling

Experiences

Spiritual:_____

_____

Painful:_____

_____

Educational:_____

_____

Ministry:_____

_____

Other circumstances that may impact my service:

_____

_____

_____

_____

Take Home Page NATURE

DAILY READINGS AND REFLECTIONS

We may be unable to change our present circumstances, and certainly we can't change our past experiences. But God will produce joy and peace within us as we serve Him—regardless of our present or our past. Let's conclude with more Scriptures about His joy and peace.

Monday—Read Luke 2:10-12. Angels bring good news of great joy.
Tuesday—Read Luke 24:45-53. Jesus leaves the disciples with joy.
Wednesday—Read John 15:5-11. Jesus reveals the true way to joy.
Thursday—Read John 14:23-27. Instruction from the Holy Spirit and peace from Jesus.
Friday—Read Philippians 4:4-8. Rejoicing in the Lord brings peace.
Saturday—Read James 3:13-18. Wisdom from heaven brings peace.

COMPLETE THE BLANKS

Can you complete the acronym for the five elements we've studied?

S _____ Gifts
H _____ Causes And Motivations
A _____
P _____ Style
E _____

HOW'S YOUR WHEELS?

Using the four types of experiences, compare your life to a car.

SPIRITUAL EXPERIENCES: How's my motor running? Have I turned on the ignition? How's my upkeep? (Meaningful decisions and times with God.)

PAINFUL EXPERIENCES: Had any accidents? Any major mechanical breakdowns? (Problems, hurts, trials God has used to mold me.)

EDUCATIONAL EXPERIENCES: What upgrades have I had? Extra options? (Favorite school subjects, courses in areas of special interest, self-study or practice, specialized education or training.)

MINISTRY EXPERIENCES: What's my mileage? Where have I been, and where am I going? (Areas of past service, ministry accomplishments.)